KW-481-026

Contents

50p

Cordon Bleu

Poultry
and Game

Cordon Bleu

Poultry
and Game

SPHERE BOOKS LIMITED
30/32 Grays Inn Road, London, WC1X 8JL

First published in Great Britain in 1972 by
B.P.C. Publishing Ltd.

© B.P.C. Publishing Ltd., 1972

First Sphere edition 1973

Designed by Melvyn Kyte
Printed by Waterlow (Dunstable) Ltd.

ISBN 0 7221 2513 5

These recipes have been adapted from the Cordon Bleu Cookery Course
published by Purnell in association with the London Cordon Bleu
Cookery School
Principal : Rosemary Hume ; Co-Principal : Muriel Downes
Quantities given are enough for 4 servings unless more are specified.
Spoon measures are level unless otherwise stated.

Introduction

Poultry is a term referring to all the farmyard fowl bred specially for eating. These birds provide an endless variety of dishes ; many are classics to those who love good food, but there is also room for considerable experiment by an adventurous Cordon Bleu cook.

Game, on the other hand, is essentially free. This freedom is protected by law and there are 'close' seasons when game birds and animals may not be shot. The seasons are determined by the breeding habits of the different creatures, and by their growth rates — so game may not be killed during the various breeding seasons, nor while the young are being reared. You will find that the seasons vary slightly from time to time, and from one part of the country to another, but those we have given are a current guide.

The flavour of all these birds and animals is affected by what they feed on. On the farm this is controllable ; nowadays there are certain standard feeds and the flavours of poultry will vary little unless you go somewhere where the fowl still run free and fend for themselves. Game on the other hand may feed on the young, tender shoots of the highland moors or the richer grains and grasses of East Anglia — and the flavour will reflect this difference. Wild duck may even have a slightly fishy flavour. This is one of the joys of game — it is a continuous gastronomic experiment, for you never know quite what to expect !

You can of course buy poultry and game ready prepared, like any other meat. But if you live in the country, or have friends who do, you are equally likely to be presented with the whole thing, freshly killed and still furred or feathered. For these occasions it is as well to be prepared, and alongside our favourite Cordon Bleu recipes we have included in this book details of how to pluck, skin, draw and joint.

Rosemary Hume
Muriel Downes

Chicken and turkey

The mild and tender chicken, subtle flavoured, will grace your table economically for family or formal meals.
Roast or braised, boiled, casseroled or fried, you can eat chicken a hundred different ways and never tire of the flavour.
Its larger cousin, the turkey, is a traditional Christmas feast and the young birds are well worth remembering for other special occasions.

Types of chicken

These vary considerably in size and flavour according to age.

Poussins are baby chickens (4-6 weeks old) usually sufficient for only one person. Double poussins (6-10 weeks old) are slightly larger and will serve two. Poussins are best roasted, pot roasted or grilled.

Spring chickens (broilers) are birds about 3 months old, weighing 2-2$\frac{1}{2}$ lb. They may be roasted or pot roasted and are ideal for a sauté as the joints are not too large. One bird is sufficient for 3-4 people, depending on the method of cooking.

Roasters average 3-4 lb and are birds about 6-12 months old. This is the most popular size chicken for a family and may be roasted, boiled or pot roasted, and served with an appropriate sauce and garnish.

Boilers are chickens of 12 months and over, weighing about 4-6 lb. They are used for making broths, for cold dishes or mousses, or served with a sauce. They are usually meaty but inclined to fat.

Boilers should be simmered for 2-3 hours in water with root vegetables and a bouquet garni to flavour; add also a little salt and a few peppercorns. Keep the liquid well skimmed of fat and the pan covered. Cool chicken a little in the liquid before taking out for carving. As the skin is inclined to be thick it is best removed just before serving.

Capons are young cockerels treated by injection and then specially fattened for the table. They usually weigh 5-8 lb and are good for a large family meal. They can be roasted or poached for about 2 hours for use as a cold buffet dish.

French roasting is a good method of cooking chicken, duck or turkey, particularly if the bird is to be served cold, because the flesh remains succulent and full of flavour. The bird is roasted in butter with a little strong stock (as opposed to English roasting, when dripping only is used, which is apt to make the flesh dry). Full instructions for French roasting are given in the recipe for Chicken Véronique, page 22.

Poultry is often bought already trussed, but a recipe may require a bird to be trussed after it has been boned and stuffed so that its shape is kept during cooking. Step-by-step diagrams of trussing and carving are given on the following pages.

Preparation

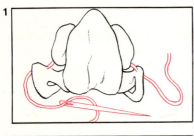

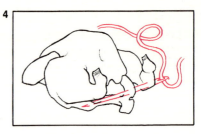

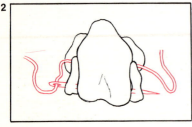

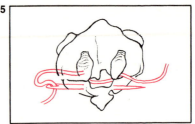

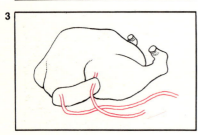

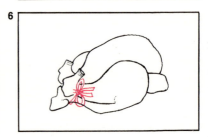

Trussing a chicken

Fold flap of skin over back of neck end, fold ends of wing pinions backwards and under to hold neck skin in position. Place bird on back, press legs down into sides to plump breast. Thread trussing needle with stout thread or string

1 Insert trussing needle through wing joint nearest you, then through thigh and body to emerge in same position on far side

2 Re-insert needle into other end of this joint (leaving a stitch showing 1-2 inches long, depending on size of joint) and pass back through body and out at corresponding part of the other wing joint

3 Tie the two thread ends in a bow

4 Re-thread needle, insert through skin at end of one drumstick, through gristle at either side of parson's nose, and out through skin of other drumstick end

5 Re-insert needle in carcass under drumsticks and draw through

6 Tie the two thread ends firmly at side

(Alternatively use a skewer and string. Push skewer through bird below thigh bone, turn on to its breast. Catch in wing pinions, pass string under ends of skewer and cross pinions over its back. Turn bird over, bring up string to secure drumsticks, and tie it round parson's nose)

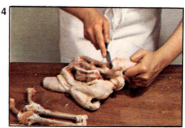

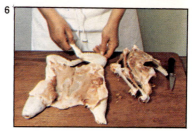

Boning a chicken

1 *Remove the trussing string. With a sharp knife, slit the skin down the underside of the bird. Work skin and flesh from the carcass with the knife until the leg joint is reached*
2 *Nick sinew between ball and socket joint joining thigh bone to carcass ; hold end of joint in one hand, and working from inside of leg, cut away flesh. Scrape thigh bone clean*
3 *Then continue cleaning the drumstick until the whole leg bone is free of flesh. Now remove the leg bone from carcass. Repeat this cleaning process with the other leg*
4 *Sever the wing joint from the carcass. Still using the knife, work*
down towards and on to the breastbone; stop there. Free the other wing in the same way*
5 *Now very carefully cut away the skin from the top of the breastbone. Take great care not to split the skin and to keep both sides of the chicken attached so that it remains in one piece for stuffing*
6 *Lay the chicken flat ready for stuffing to be spread over cut surfaces. Then sew up or secure with poultry pins/lacers ; truss in the usual way (see opposite)*

Jointing a chicken

1 Hold chicken firmly on board with one hand. With sharp knife, saw away skin between leg and breast. Then, pressing flat of knife against carcass, take leg in other hand and bend it outwards until the oyster bone breaks away from carcass

2 Slide the knife around the leg joint cutting down towards the 'parson's nose', keeping it between the oyster and backbone. Leg is now severed from the carcass and has the oyster bone attached. Cut off the other leg in same way

3 Now make a slantwise cut with knife half-way up the breast across to the top of wishbone from the neck end, to end of the wing joints. With scissors, cut down through wishbone and ribs to detach the wing with a good portion of breast

4 Twist the wing pinion out and tuck it under this breast meat to hold the joint flat. This makes for even browning of the meat. To get both wings of even size, make the slantwise cuts at the same time. Detach other wing in the same way

5 Cut away the breast meat in one piece with the scissors. All that is now left of the carcass are the ribs, the backbone and parson's nose

6 The joints are now ready for cooking. The carcass may be cut in half and then sautéd with the chicken joints to give the finished dish additional flavour

Splitting a poussin

(see photographs on page 44)

1 Hold bird firmly on board with one hand, make a cut with a sharp knife through skin and flesh on top of the breast.
2 Split in half with scissors, starting at wishbone end, and cutting through on one side of backbone. When divided, trim away backbone from the other half of the poussin.
3 Trim off the knuckle bones and end wing pinions after grilling.

To split a cooked poussin
Lift bird carefully from pan on to a board. Cut and draw out trussing strings before splitting as above.

Boning a poussin

A bird can be completely boned out and then stuffed, but a better shape is obtained if it is only partially boned, with leg and breastbone left in for a young poussin, but breastbone removed from an older one. This makes trussing easier.
1 Remove trussing strings, turn bird on to breastbone ; with a small, sharp knife, slit skin down underside of bird.
2 With tail of bird towards you, ease flesh and skin away from carcass on left-hand side. Work evenly, with short, sharp strokes (keep knife edge against ribs). Sever leg and wing through the ball and socket joints.
3 Turn bird round, lift skin and flesh off other side, sever the joints as before.

4 Cut away the rib and back-bone with the scissors.
5 Bird is now ready to have stuffing spread over cut surfaces. Sew up underside, or secure with poultry pins / lacers, and truss.

Plucking

To pluck poultry, place a large sheet of paper or a large container under the bird, away from any draught. Hold the bird firmly, and sharply pull out a few feathers at a time in the direction opposite to that in which they lie. Particular care should be exercised on the breast feathers, otherwise the flesh will tear.

To pluck the wing feathers, bend wing into a natural position. Grip all of the main feathers in one hand and then give them a sharp pull — this will extend the wing, and nearly all the feathers will come out in one go. Then pull out the remaining feathers one at a time ; you may need to use pliers.

When all the feathers are removed, singe off the remaining down with a lighted taper or swing the bird over an open gas flame.

Poultry should be hung either before or after plucking for 2-3 days as this improves the flavour and the texture. Plucking is more easily done while the bird is still warm. Draw as for game, see page 96.

▶ 15

Preparation continued

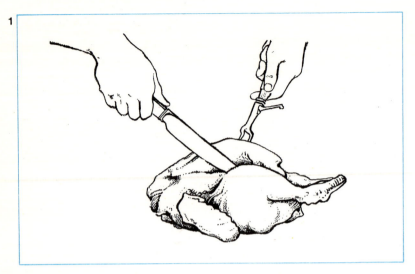

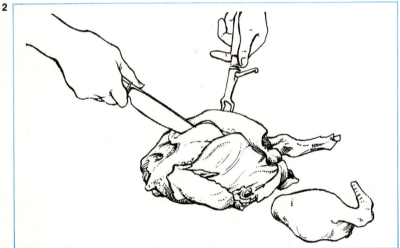

Carving a chicken

1 Hold bird firmly with carving fork through to back, cut skin around leg, place knife between leg and carcass, press gently outwards to expose joint ; cut through, slip knife point under back to release the oyster (choice meat on carcass bone) with thigh

2 With knife at top end of breast-bone opposite where breast and wishbone meet, cut down parallel to one side of wishbone for a good slice of breast with the wing

3

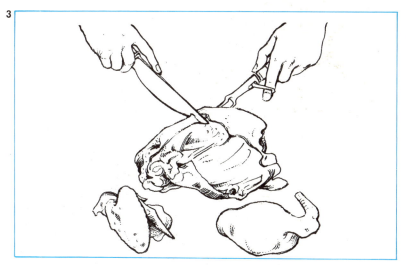

4

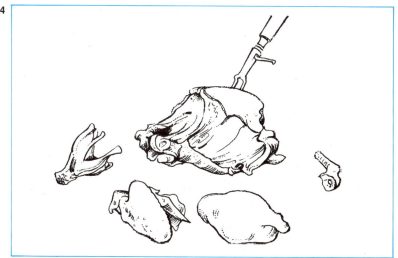

3 & 4 *Similar pieces are carved from other side of bird. Cut off wishbone by carving behind it down the front of carcass. Carve remaining breast into good slices. (With a large chicken, divide leg into two for good portion of thigh meat with drumstick. Cut through bone with kitchen scissors with half-hole in them)*

Cold roast chicken Mojibi

1 roasting chicken (weighing 3-3½ lb)
1½-2 oz butter
sprig of rosemary
salt and pepper
½ pint chicken stock (made from giblets) see page 156
1 pint aspic jelly — see page 150
watercress (to garnish)

Method

Set the oven at 400°F or Mark 6.

Rub the chicken well with butter and put a good nut of it inside the bird with the rosemary and seasoning. Place chicken in a roasting tin with half the stock ; cover with a buttered paper and roast for about 1 hour, basting from time to time (a frozen bird will take a little longer). The chicken should be well browned on all sides.

Watchpoint To make sure that your chicken is browned to perfection and keeps a good shape for carving, start cooking with the bird lying on its back. After the first basting, ie. after about 20 minutes cooking time, turn the bird on to its side. When well coloured, turn it on to the other side, baste again and continue cooking, breast side uppermost.

Take up the chicken, tip the remaining stock into the roasting tin and boil up well ; taste for seasoning. Strain liquid through a piece of muslin into a small bowl, leave to cool and when set remove the fat from the top.

When the chicken is quite cold, carve and arrange joints on a serving dish ; cooking juices may be spooned between the joints. Baste with the very cold but still liquid aspic jelly and leave to set. Garnish with bouquets of watercress and serve with rice salad (see page 155) and a green salad of your choice.

Turning the chicken after the first basting to ensure even browning

Arranging cold cooked chicken joints before coating with cool aspic jelly

Chicken béarnais

2 ½ lb chicken
1-2 oz butter, or bacon fat
1 large onion
4 oz gammon rasher (in the piece)
6-8 baby carrots
1 wineglass white wine, or chicken
  stock (see page 156)
3 large tomatoes
2 cloves of garlic
salt and pepper
2 tablespoons double cream
  (optional)
chopped parsley — to garnish

The Béarn province in the French Pyrenees is well known for its good food and local wines.

Method

Set oven at 350°F or Mark 4. Joint the chicken ; when jointing a whole bird for a casserole, put in the back for extra flavour, especially if you have to use water instead of stock. Fry joints slowly in the fat until golden-brown, then take out.

Slice onion thinly, cut bacon into squares, blanch both in cold water (bring to boil and drain). Quarter and blanch carrots, lay them in bottom of casserole. Arrange chicken on top, together with onion and bacon. Moisten with wine, or stock, season lightly, cover and cook gently for 1 hour in pre-set oven.

Skin and slice tomatoes (see page 156), flick out seeds, add flesh to casserole with garlic crushed with salt. Cover, replace in oven. Continue to cook for 15 minutes or until chicken and carrots are tender. Take out the back of chicken before serving.

Finish, if wished, with the thick cream poured over top just before serving. Dust with chopped parsley.

Boiled chicken with parsley sauce

1 large boiling fowl, or roasting
  chicken
1 large carrot (quartered)
1 large onion (quartered)
bouquet garni
6 peppercorns
½ teaspoon salt
cold water
streaky bacon rashers

For parsley sauce
2 large handfuls of fresh parsley
¾ pint milk
1 bayleaf
1 blade of mace
6 peppercorns
1 ½ oz butter
2 rounded tablespoons plain flour
salt and pepper

Boiling is an economical and suitable way of cooking a chicken too old for roasting, because the long, slow cooking makes it tender.

Method

Set the bird on its back in a large saucepan. Surround with the quartered vegetables, add the bouquet garni, peppercorns and salt. For a boiling fowl pour in enough water barely to cover ; for a roasting chicken, sufficient just to cover the thighs. Cover saucepan and bring slowly to the boil. Simmer boiling fowl for 2-3 hours until tender ; roasting fowl for 50-60 minutes. Turn bird over from time to time. When cooked, draw saucepan aside and allow to cool.

To prepare the sauce : pick parsley sprigs from stalks and wash well ; reserve some stalks. Boil sprigs for 7 minutes in a saucepan of salted water drain, press and rub through a bowl strainer to make about 1 dessertspoon of parsley purée.

Meanwhile infuse the milk with the bayleaf, mace, peppercorns, reserved parsley stalks. Strain. Melt the butter, stir in flour, blend in milk and stir until boiling. Season and simmer for 2-3 minutes, then add the parsley purée.

Remove rind from the bacon, and cut rashers in half. Grill or dry fry (see page 157) and keep hot. Take up chicken, removing the skin if using a boiling fowl.

Carve the bird and dish up. Coat with parsley sauce, garnish with bacon, and serve separately any remaining sauce. Serve boiled rice (see page 28) or creamed potatoes (see page 153) with this dish.

Chicken Véronique with julienne potato cake

3-3½ lb roasting chicken
salt and pepper
2 oz butter
3-4 sprigs tarragon
½ pint chicken stock (see page 156)
½-1 teaspoon arrowroot
2-3 tablespoons double cream
4 oz muscat, or other white grapes (peeled and pipped)
squeeze of lemon juice

Method

Set oven at 400°F or Mark 6. Wipe the chicken inside with a damp cloth but do not wash the bird as this would hinder browning and do nothing to improve its flavour. Season inside as this will penetrate the flesh, whereas seasoning on the outside only would not, and the salt would draw out the juices and prevent browning.

If the bird is not already trussed by the poulterer, do this yourself, as a well-trussed bird not only keeps a better shape in cooking but consequently is easier to carve.

Rub the chicken well with 2 oz of butter, putting a good nut of this inside with the tarragon and seasoning. Place the chicken, breast side up, in the roasting tin, with half of the chicken stock. Cover with buttered paper. Roast for about 1 hour in pre-set oven.

After the first 15-20 minutes, when the flesh should be set but not coloured, baste and turn on one side. Baste and turn again after another 15-20 minutes and finish off with breast side up again, removing the buttered paper for the last few minutes of roasting. The chicken should be well browned on all sides.

To test if the chicken is done, take a cooking knife with a fine point (or even a hat pin) and pierce the flesh of the thigh. The liquid that runs out should be quite clear ; continue cooking if it is at all pink. A frozen bird usually takes longer to cook and colour because the skin is so wet.

When cooked, take chicken out of oven, carve on a wooden board and keep hot. If, at the end of cooking time, the juices in the pan have not cooked down to a glaze (a sticky consistency), put tin over steady heat on top of stove leaving juices and butter to reduce until brown and sticky. Then add remaining ¼ pint of stock to make gravy.

Scrape the pan well with the basting spoon and strain mixture into a small saucepan. To thicken slightly, so as to bind the butter into the stock, add ½-1 teaspoon of arrowroot (mixed with 1 tablespoon of stock or water). Add this away from the heat and then stir until boiling. It needs no further cooking and will be quite clear. Mix in the cream, adjust the seasoning to taste, and keep hot.

If grapes are difficult to peel, scald by pouring water over them, count 12, then replace hot water with cold. Then peel and pip them, cover with a little lemon juice and wet, grease-proof paper to keep out air until they are needed.

When chicken, gravy and potatoes are ready to be dished up, turn out the potato cake bottom side up to form a bed on which to arrange the served pieces of chicken. Put grapes in the gravy and then spoon, with as much liquid as comes with them, over the chicken. Serve the rest of the gravy separately in a sauce boat, otherwise the potatoes will soak up the sauce. Serve with a green salad.

Chicken Véronique is a classic dish, the bird being French roast with a grape garnish. Serve it on top of the julienne potato cake (see page 24 for recipe and photograph) ▶

Julienne potato cake

1 lb potatoes (peeled)
1 oz butter
salt and pepper

Method

Although the potatoes may be peeled ahead of time, they must never be cut into strips until you are ready to cook them. Soaking in water removes a certain amount of their starch which is needed to knit them together. As they cook, the steam and starch combine and, when tender, the potato cake is easy to remove from the pan in which it is cooked.

While the chicken is starting to cook, cut the peeled potatoes into julienne strips. Dry well in a cloth or absorbent kitchen paper.

Rub a thick, even coating of butter over the base and sides of a heavy 6-inch diameter frying pan, press in the potatoes, season only when a thick layer covers the base, or the salt will make the potatoes stick. All the seasoning will be absorbed by

the potatoes, none being thrown away as with the liquid from boiled potatoes.

If lid is not close-fitting, put a layer of overlapping, buttered paper between pan and lid to prevent loss of steam as this would result in potatoes over-browning or burning on the bottom before they are quite tender.

If cooked on top of stove, heat must be gentle and even (allow about 30-40 minutes). However, when entertaining, you may find it easier to combine top of stove and oven heat for cooking in following way.

Cook about 10-15 minutes on top of stove on a steady heat, testing colouring of strips by lifting lid, inserting a palette knife down side and taking a quick look. With experience your nose will tell you when potatoes are coloured by the unmistakable smell of beurre noisette (butter cooked to a nut-brown). At this transfer pan to oven below chicken if oven is still set at 400°F or Mark 6, or above if chicken is cooked and oven has been turned low. Continue cooking for about 30 minutes. For final testing, use the point of a cooking knife.

If you want to make larger quantities than for 4-6 people, use 2 sandwich tins and lids made from foil with a plate on top. The pan or tin should be generously full, the weight of the plate (in the case of the tin) being used to press the potatoes down. In this case cook on top for 10 minutes only, finishing off in oven as above.

Chicken casserole with peaches

3 lb roasting chicken
2 large onions
3 oz butter
2-3 peaches (peeled and sliced)
  — preferably Hale
pinch of nutmeg
rind and juice of 1 lemon
$\frac{1}{2}$ pint chicken stock (see method, and page 156)
salt
black pepper (ground from mill)
3-4 tablespoons double cream
paprika pepper

For pilaf
8 oz long grain rice
1-2 oz onions (chopped)
1 oz butter
1 dessertspoon turmeric
1-1$\frac{1}{4}$ pints chicken stock, or water

Method

Joint the chicken neatly a few hours before cooking so that the back and trimmings can be made into stock. Finely slice the onions. Fry the chicken slowly to a golden-brown in half the butter. Melt the remaining butter in another pan, fry the onions slowly and, when turning colour, add the peaches ; continue frying over quicker heat for a few more minutes.

Put the chicken joints into the pan with the onions and peaches. Add nutmeg with two strips of pared lemon rind ; then add the stock and seasoning. Cover the pan tightly and stew chicken slowly (preferably in moderate oven pre-set at 350°F or Mark 4) for about 1 hour.

Meanwhile prepare the pilaf. Chop the onions and soften them in the butter in a flame-proof casserole. Add the rice and turmeric and fry together. Pour on the stock (or water), season well, bring to the boil, cover, and cook in the oven until the rice is tender and the stock absorbed, about 20 minutes.

When the chicken is very tender, remove it and the lemon rind from the pan. Boil up the juices in the pan, adding lemon juice to taste, and adjust the seasoning. Stir in the cream and boil sauce rapidly until it coats the back of a spoon.

Dish up the chicken, pour over the sauce, dust with paprika pepper and serve the pilaf separately.

Chicken casserole italienne

$3\frac{1}{2}$ lb roasting chicken
1 oz butter
1 onion (finely chopped)
4 teaspoons tomato purée
$\frac{1}{2}$ pint chicken stock (made from the
   giblets — see page 156)
salt and pepper
bouquet garni
1 teaspoon cornflour, or arrowroot
1 can ($7\frac{1}{2}$ oz) button mushrooms
2 oz cooked ham (shredded)
chopped parsley — to garnish

Carefully brown chicken and onion before adding tomato purée and stock

Method

Brown the chicken on all sides in the butter in a large flame-proof casserole. Allow at least 10 minutes for this as the chicken has little or no fat between the skin and flesh and, if browned quickly, tends to become dry. Always start by browning the breast, first on one side and then the other and finish with the back or under-side. In this way there is no danger of the breast getting discoloured or damaged should the butter start to overbrown, and your chicken will be the right way up for cooking.

Add the onion to the casserole and continue cooking slowly until golden-brown ; blend in the tomato purée and stock, season, add the herbs and bring to the boil. Cover the casserole tightly and continue cooking slowly on top of the stove or in the oven, pre-set at 350°F or Mark 4, until the bird is tender — about 50-60 minutes. Take out the chicken and keep hot while you thicken the sauce in the casserole with the cornflour, or arrowroot, mixed to a paste with 1 tablespoon stock or water, and boil up well. Add the mushrooms and ham.

Carve the chicken into neat joints and put back in the casserole. Finish with chopped parsley and serve.

The chicken, carved into joints for serving, is sprinkled with parsley

Curried chicken with boiled rice

3½ lb roasting chicken
2 tablespoons oil
2 onions (chopped)
1 tablespoon ground coriander
1 teaspoon cumin
1 teaspoon chilli powder
½ teaspoon turmeric
1 dessertspoon coconut cream
1 dessertspoon tamarind
  (infused in 1 cup of water)
3 tomatoes

This spiced Indian chicken is hot and the quantity of chilli powder can be cut down. If spices are unobtainable, use a good quality curry powder. The coconut cream and tamarind may be replaced by 1-2 tablespoons desiccated coconut or ground almond infused in 1 cup of boiling water. This dish can easily be kept hot, or can be prepared early and reheated.

Method

Joint the chicken and fry gently in a pan with the oil until golden-brown. Remove joints from the pan and put in the onions ; cook very slowly until golden-brown.

Mix the spices together, add to the pan and continue cooking for 1-2 minutes. Stir in the coconut cream and tamarind infusion and bring to the boil. Put the chicken back in the pan, season with a little salt and simmer, covered, for 15-20 minutes.

Scald and peel the tomatoes (see page 156), then cut into quarters, remove the seeds and chop the flesh finely ; add to the pan, and continue cooking until the chicken is tender (about 15 minutes). Trim the joints, if necessary.

Serve with boiled rice.

Boiled rice

There are almost as many ways of cooking rice as there are cooks, so if you have your own well-tried method stick to it, but if you have problems, the following method is foolproof.

Allow 2 oz of washed rice per person.

Shower the rice into a large pan of boiling, salted water, at least 3 quarts for 8 oz, and add a slice of lemon for flavour. Stir with a fork to prevent sticking and boil steadily for about 12 minutes until tender. Rice very quickly overcooks so watch its cooking time carefully.

To stop rice cooking, tip it quickly into a colander and drain, or pour ½ cup of cold water into the pan and drain in a colander. Then pour over a jug of hot water to wash away any remaining starch, making several holes through the rice (with the handle of a wooden spoon) to help it drain more quickly. Turn on to a large meat dish and leave in a warm place to dry.

Turn rice from time to time with a fork.

For easy reheating, spoon rice into a well-buttered, shallow ovenproof dish which should be small enough for the rice to fill it amply. Place a sheet of well-buttered paper over the top. The rice can then be reheated and served in this dish. Allow 30 minutes in the oven at 350°F or Mark 4.

The chicken joints are fried in oil until golden, and then spices are added to make a hot curry

Curried chicken with peaches

3 ½ lb roasting chicken
2 tablespoons olive oil, or butter
1 medium-size onion (finely chopped)
1 rounded tablespoon curry powder
1 rounded tablespoon plain flour
¾ pint chicken stock (made from the giblets, see page 156)
1 clove of garlic (crushed with ½ teaspoon salt)
¼ pint nut milk (see below right)
1 tablespoon redcurrant jelly (see page 154) or juice of ½ lemon mixed with 1 dessertspoon sugar
3-4 tablespoons double cream
1 teaspoon arrowroot (optional)
2 fresh white-fleshed peaches (peeled and sliced)

To serve
8 oz rice (boiled)

Trimming the casseroled chicken joints before adding the curry sauce

Method

Joint the chicken, leaving plenty of carcass bone to prevent the flesh shrinking, and brown it slowly in half the oil (or butter) in a flameproof casserole. Remove chicken joints from the casserole and keep warm.

Heat the remaining oil (or butter), add the onion and cook gently until it is just turning colour. Stir in the curry powder and continue cooking for 2-3 minutes. Dust in the flour and cook for 1 minute. Draw casserole away from the heat and gradually add the stock, then stir in the garlic and allow to simmer for 20 minutes. Put the chicken back in the casserole, cover tightly and continue cooking on top of the stove or in the oven, pre-set at 325°F or Mark 3, for about 45 minutes until tender. Trim the chicken joints and strain the sauce from the casserole into a pan. Add the nut milk with the redcurrant jelly (or lemon juice and sugar) to sauce, simmer it for 2-3 minutes.

Wipe out the casserole and replace the chicken. Add the cream to the sauce and thicken, if necessary, with arrowroot slaked with a little stock or water. Spoon curry sauce over the chicken and reheat carefully. About 10-15 minutes before serving, add peaches. Serve boiled rice separately.

Nut milk. To make ¼ pint of this milk, infuse 2 tablespoons ground almonds or desiccated coconut in 1 teacup of boiling water for 1 hour. Then strain liquid before use.

Chicken provençale with saffron rice

3 lb roasting chicken, or chicken
joints
2 oz butter
4 cloves of garlic (unpeeled)
6 large tomatoes
1 wineglass sherry, or brandy
1 teaspoon tomato purée
salt and pepper
1 tablespoon mixed herbs (chopped)

Some aromatic herbs, such as marjoram, oregano, thyme or basil, can be used in this dish but they must be mixed with parsley in the proportion of one-third aromatic herbs to two-thirds parsley. Oregano is wild marjoram.

Method

If using a whole chicken, joint it.

Melt butter in a frying pan, add unpeeled garlic cloves and chicken joints, skin-side down, and cook slowly for about 15 minutes until joints are half cooked.

Meanwhile, scald and skin the tomatoes (see page 156), remove seeds and chop flesh very finely.

Turn the chicken over at this half-cooked stage, remove garlic and pour in sherry or brandy. Set this alight and when the alcohol has burnt out, simmer until all the liquid has evaporated. The chicken should look brown and sticky at this stage. Add the tomato flesh, tomato purée and seasoning to the pan and continue cooking for about 15 minutes until chicken is tender and the tomatoes well reduced.

Remove chicken from pan, trim joints by cutting away any excess bone showing after the natural shrinkage of flesh has taken place during cooking and arrange in a serving dish. Boil remaining tomato mixture to reduce further, then pour it over the chicken and sprinkle with chopped herbs.

Serve with saffron rice (see right) and a green salad, or French beans.

Chicken joints are flamed in sherry or brandy for this dish and served with saffron rice and green salad

Saffron rice

8 oz long grain rice
pinch of saffron (soaked in 1
eggcup of boiling water)
4 rashers of streaky bacon
1 oz butter
1 small onion (finely sliced)
salt and pepper

Method

Cook the rice in plenty of boiling, salted water for about 12 minutes or until tender. Turn into a colander and rinse with a jug of hot water. Leave to drain thoroughly.

Meanwhile, remove rind from bacon. Melt butter in a saucepan, add bacon and fry until brown and crisp. Lift from the pan with a draining spoon and, when cool, crush into small pieces. Add finely sliced onion to the pan and cook slowly until golden-brown ; fork in the rice and saffron. Toss over heat, adding extra butter if necessary. Season and stir in bacon.

This rich tomato-flavoured chicken provençale is sprinkled with aromatic herbs before serving and is accompanied by saffron rice

Poussins sauté au citron

2 double poussins
1½ oz butter
salt and pepper
1 wineglass white wine
¼ pint strong chicken stock (see page 156)
piece of glaze (size of a walnut) — see note

Method

Split the poussins. Melt the butter in a sauté pan, put in the birds and allow them to brown slowly on both sides. Then season well, add the wine and stock, cover and simmer for a further 15 minutes. Take up the birds, add the glaze to the liquor in the pan, reduce it and pour over the chicken. Garnish with lemon fritters (see right) ; serve with new potatoes tossed in butter and chopped parsley.

Note : as it takes so much first-class bone stock to make even

Poussins sauté au citron, served with lemon fritters and new potatoes

a very small quantity of glaze, this is very difficult to make at home. If you take a cake of beef dripping and turn it upside down, you will find at the bottom a little layer of good dark brown jelly. 1-2 teaspoons of this jelly would be sufficient for this dish.

Lemon fritters

Boil 2 lemons for 20-30 minutes. Drain, cut into quarters or slices. Marinate in French dressing, then dip them in fritter batter made with 4 tablespoons plain flour, pinch of salt, 2 egg yolks, 1 tablespoon melted butter, $\frac{1}{4}$ pint milk and 1 egg white. Fry in deep fat.

Poussins Valentino

3 double poussins
2 oz butter
salt and pepper
grated rind and juice of $\frac{1}{2}$ lemon
$\frac{1}{4}$ pint strong chicken stock (see page 156)
1 teaspoon arrowroot (slaked with a little water)
$\frac{1}{4}$ pint double cream
$\frac{1}{4}$ lb button mushrooms
1 small bunch of asparagus
1 oz Parmesan cheese (grated)

You may add 2-3 oz sliced and shredded ham to the sauce, with the asparagus and mushrooms.

Method
Melt $1\frac{1}{2}$ oz of the butter in a large pan, put in the poussins, seasoning and a good squeeze of lemon juice with a little of the grated rind. Brown lightly, then cover the pan and cook gently for 25-30 minutes, shaking the pan frequently and turning the birds over once or twice. To keep birds moist during cooking, add 1-2 tablespoons stock, if necessary. Remove poussins and keep hot.

Add any remaining stock to the pan, thicken slightly with a little slaked arrowroot, tip on the cream, bring to the boil, seasoning well.

Cook the mushrooms quickly in the remaining butter and a squeeze of lemon juice. Trim and tie asparagus in bundles and cook in boiling salted water for about 20 minutes.

Split the poussins, add the mushrooms and asparagus tips to the sauce and spoon it over the poussins. Scatter a little Parmesan cheese over the top and brown them under grill.

Suprêmes of chicken Villeroi

6 suprêmes of uncooked chicken
2-3 tablespoons white wine

For duxelles stuffing
1 shallot (finely chopped)
1 oz butter
6 oz flat mushrooms
2 tablespoons fresh white breadcrumbs
1 egg white
3 oz raw chicken (minced)
salt
3-4 tablespoons double cream

For duchesse potato mixture
1½ lb potatoes
½ oz butter
salt and pepper
grate of nutmeg
1 egg yolk
2-3 tablespoons hot milk
1 egg (beaten) — for brushing

For sauce
1 oz butter
¾ oz plain flour
½ pint strong chicken stock (see
page 156)
salt and pepper
liaison of 2 egg yolks and ¼ pint
single cream
squeeze of lemon juice
¼ oz butter (to finish)

6 large rounds of buttered greaseproof
paper, or foil ; forcing bag, plain
pipe and vegetable rose pipe

Cut the suprêmes (as shown in photograph), and for this recipe cut off the pinion and remove the skin.

The drum stick and thigh joints from one chicken will give you enough raw chicken for mincing ; the remaining joints can be made into a casserole or pie.

Method
First prepare the duxelles stuffing : put the shallot in a pan with the butter, cover pan and cook shallot very slowly until it is soft but not coloured. Wash the mushrooms in salted water, chop them finely and add to shallot in the pan ; cook them briskly for 2-3 minutes to drive off any moisture, then stir in the breadcrumbs. Turn mixture on to a plate to cool. Whisk the egg white until frothy, then beat it into the minced chicken a little at a time ; add salt, followed by the cream, then work in the mushroom mixture. Taste for seasoning.

Set oven at 350°F or Mark 4. Split the suprêmes very carefully just above the natural division. Put the stuffing in the forcing bag, fitted with the plain pipe, and fill the suprêmes. Set each suprême on a round of buttered paper or foil and sprinkle with a little white wine ; seal the edges of the paper to make 'papillotes' (envelopes). Cook in pre-set oven for 45-50 minutes.

Meanwhile make the duchesse potato mixture : boil the potatoes until tender, drain and dry them well, then pass them through a potato ricer or Mouli sieve. Return potato to the saucepan, beat in the butter, seasonings, egg yolk and enough hot milk to make a firm purée. Put mixture into forcing bag, fitted with the vegetable rose pipe, and make a border of potato round the edge of a large gratin dish ; brush with the beaten egg and put dish in the oven, above the chicken, and allow to brown.

To prepare the sauce : make a roux with the butter and flour and cook it gently to a pale straw colour. Tip on the stock, stir until boiling, then simmer for 5 minutes ; season. Add the liaison of egg yolks and cream, reheat carefully, then add the lemon juice ; adjust the seasoning and beat in the extra $\frac{1}{4}$ oz butter.

Take the suprêmes out of the oven, remove them from the paper 'envelopes' and place them in the gratin dish, inside the potato border ; spoon over enough sauce to coat the suprêmes. Serve the rest of the sauce in a gravy boat and hand French beans separately.

For suprêmes, wing and breast are removed from the uncooked chicken in one piece, with a filleting knife

After chicken suprêmes have been split, they are filled with stuffing mixture and placed on rounds of foil

Suprêmes of chicken Villeroi

continued

Suprêmes of chicken in a creamy sauce are bordered with duchesse potato

Chicken waterzoi

1 roasting chicken (weighing 3 lb)
3 young carrots
1 medium-size onion
2 leeks
1 oz butter
salt and pepper
pinch of sugar
2 wineglasses white wine
4 parsley roots (Hamburg
  parsley if possible)
$\frac{1}{2}$-$\frac{3}{4}$ pint chicken stock (see page 156)
2 teaspoons arrowroot
2 egg yolks
3-4 fl oz double cream
chopped chervil and tarragon

This dish is Flemish in origin and the name is derived from waterzootje, which is in fact a fish dish, but chicken waterzoi is prepared in the same way.

Method

Set oven at 350°F or Mark 4.

Cut the vegetables in julienne strips (about $\frac{1}{8}$ inch by 1$\frac{1}{2}$ inches long). Melt half the butter in a small flameproof pan and add the vegetables ; cover and cook for 1 minute, then season lightly and add the sugar. Pour over 1 glass of wine and bring to the boil ; cover with a buttered paper and lid and cook in a pre-set moderate oven until the wine has evaporated (about 10 minutes).

Wash and scrape the parsley roots well and tie them together with string. Season inside the bird with salt and pepper and truss neatly. Rub the remaining butter round the sides of a deep flameproof casserole, put in the chicken, pour over the rest of the wine and the stock and set the parsley roots alongside. Season with salt and pepper and scatter the vegetables over the chicken ; cover with a buttered paper and close-fitting lid and bring to the boil. Turn the oven down to 325°F or Mark 3 and cook the chicken until it is very tender (about 1-1$\frac{1}{2}$ hours).

Take up the chicken, cut it into neat joints and arrange in a deep serving dish. Lift out the parsley roots, rub them through a wire strainer and return this purée to the casserole. Mix the arrowroot with the egg yolks and add the cream ; stir this into the vegetables and stock and cook gently until sauce coats a wooden spoon. Taste for seasoning, spoon sauce over chicken.

Chicken with truffle

1 large broad-breasted chicken
1 fresh truffle
sprig of thyme
small bayleaf
salt and pepper
1-2 pieces of fresh pork fat (large enough to wrap round the chicken)
2 tablespoons brandy
1 wineglass Madeira

Method

Set oven at 350°F or Mark 4.

Wash and scrape the truffle, trim to a neat oval and cut in thin slices. Reserve the trimmings. Work the slices of truffle between the skin and flesh of the chicken's breast, tuck the herbs inside the chicken and season. Wrap the chicken in pork fat and then in a sheet of buttered greaseproof paper and tie with string. Cook in pre-set moderate oven, allowing 18-20 minutes per lb. About 10 minutes before you think the bird is ready, remove the paper and the pork fat, baste well with the liquid in the pan and return bird to oven to colour lightly. Check to see if the bird is cooked by piercing the thigh with a trussing needle. If the liquid that runs is pink, give it another 10 minutes' cooking.

Then take up the bird, remove the string, cut off the wing pinions and trim the drum sticks. Set on a hot platter. Skim off any fat in the pan, add the brandy and Madeira and boil up well, then strain. Return liquid to pan with the reserved chopped trimmings of truffle and simmer for 1 minute ; spoon this over the chicken and serve.

Chicken Marengo

1 roasting chicken (weighing 2½-3 lb)
1 tablespoon oil
2 oz clarified butter
2 large ripe tomatoes
1 clove of garlic (crushed with a little salt)
1 tablespoon tomato purée
1 wineglass white wine
½ pint demi-glace sauce (see page 73)
12 small button mushrooms

To garnish
1 small egg per person
1 heart-shaped croûte per person
chopped parsley
1 crayfish tail per person

Heart-shaped croûtes are dipped in sauce and chopped parsley before the eggs are placed on them to garnish the chicken Marengo

Method

Joint the chicken, heat the oil, add the butter and put in the chicken, skin side down ; cook slowly until golden-brown on both sides. Remove from the pan, cover and keep warm.

Tip the fat from the pan and keep it on one side to cook the croûtes and eggs. Scald and skin the tomatoes (see page 156), cut them in four, squeeze out the seeds and chop the flesh. Put these in the sauté pan with the garlic and tomato purée. Cook over a gentle heat until well blended, add the white wine, and reduce to half quantity.

Pour on the demi-glace sauce, add the mushrooms, replace the chicken, cover and simmer gently until tender (about 25-30 minutes). Fry the croûtes and the eggs in the reserved fat.

Take up the chicken pieces, arrange them in the middle of a flat round dish and spoon over the sauce. Dip the tip of each croûte in a little sauce and then in the chopped parsley. Arrange croûtes round the dish and put a fried egg on each one. Place a crayfish tail, previously heated in a spoon or two of the stock, between each egg.

Chicken Marengo, served with fried eggs on croûtes and crayfish tails

Chicken parisienne

2½-3 lb roasting chicken
salt and pepper
2 oz butter
¼ pint chicken stock (see page 156)
⅛ pint sherry

For forcemeat
1 oz butter
1 shallot (finely chopped)
6 oz ham (minced)
6 oz veal (minced)
2-3 tablespoons fresh white bread-
    crumbs
1 dessertspoon chopped mixed
    herbs and parsley
1 egg (lightly beaten)

For velouté sauce and liaison
about 2 tablespoons plain flour
1¼ oz butter
½ pint chicken stock
1 egg yolk
¾ gill single cream
2 oz mushrooms (thinly sliced and
    cooked in ½ oz butter and squeeze
    of lemon juice)

*Poultry pins / lacers, trussing needle
and fine string*

1 *After being filled with forcemeat,
the bird is sewn up or secured with
poultry pins or lacers*
2 *The chicken is then reshaped and
trussed. Then legs are pressed well
down into the sides of the bird in
order to plump out breast*

Method

First prepare stuffing : melt butter in a saucepan, add chopped shallot, cook until soft and leave to cool. Mix the minced ham with the minced veal, breadcrumbs, herbs and parsley. Add shallot, season and bind with beaten egg.

Bone out chicken, rub inside with salt and pepper and spread with forcemeat. Sew up or secure with poultry pins / lacers, reshape and truss firmly.

Set in a roasting tin, rub bird well with butter and pour round stock and sherry. Cook in the oven, pre-set at 400° F or Mark 6, for about 1½ hours or until tender. Baste and turn every 20 minutes while cooking.

Meanwhile prepare sauce : cook flour in melted butter until lightly coloured, draw pan aside, add stock, stir until thick and boiling and simmer for 3-4 minutes, then set aside.

Make a liaison by beating egg yolk lightly and mixing cream into it. Add this to sauce, reheat carefully without boiling, and add cooked mushrooms.

When chicken is cooked, take up, remove pins and trussing string and carve. Arrange in a serving dish, spoon over a little sauce with mushrooms. Serve remaining sauce separately.

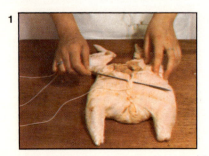

Chicken Kiev

3 roasting chickens (2½ lb each)
6 oz unsalted butter
grated rind and juice of 1 lemon
salt
black pepper (ground from mill)
pinch of ground mace, or nutmeg
chopped fresh parsley, or herbs
seasoned flour
1 egg (beaten)
dried white breadcrumbs

Deep fat bath ; cutlet frills

This is a specialised and fairly extravagant dish, but basically simple to do even though it calls for a certain amount of deftness in preparation. Once prepared, the chicken can be set aside overnight in the refrigerator to chill. It also deep-freezes well. For this recipe the whole suprême, ie. breast and wing together, is cut from the bird with the wing bone left in to give it shape. If you serve chicken Kiev at home for a party, do warn your guests to cut the chicken carefully or the butter will spurt out all over their clothes.

If making this dish it is wise to choose a recipe to prepare in the next day or so to use up the legs of the chickens, such as a casserole.

Method

Cut the suprêmes from the chickens (see photograph, page 37) ; cover the breasts with a sheet of waxed paper and bat out with a heavy knife or cutlet bat. Work the butter with the lemon rind and juice, seasoning, mace (or nutmeg) and parsley (or herbs) and put in refrigerator until very hard. Cut the hard butter into six finger-length pieces.

Put a piece of butter on each suprême, fold in the sides and roll up. Roll in seasoned flour, brush with beaten egg and roll in the breadcrumbs, pressing these on well. Allow to dry.
Note : at this stage the suprêmes may be refrigerated or deep-frozen. If they are frozen, thaw them in the refrigerator for 6-7 hours before frying.

Heat the fat to 380°F (oil to 375°F) and fry the chicken until golden-brown ; allow 4-6 minutes for this. Drain, put a cutlet frill on the wing bone and serve very hot. This quantity allows for two second helpings.

1 *For chicken Kiev, suprême is wrapped round chilled herb butter*
2 *The folded chicken is rolled in seasoned flour, brushed with egg and the crumbs are pressed on well*

Spring chicken alsacienne

3 **double poussins**
1 **tablespoon oil**
1 **oz butter**
salt and pepper
1½ **wineglasses Alsatian white wine**
1 **teaspoon arrowroot**
¼ **pint strong chicken stock (made from the giblets and bones)**
1 **small can (2½ oz) pâté de foie**
3 **tablespoons double cream**
watercress (to garnish)

This quantity of poussins allows for some second helpings.

Method

Split the poussins and cut away the backbone and rib-cage ; put these to cook in a pan, with the giblets and water to cover, to make stock.

Heat the oil in sauté pan or shallow casserole, add the butter and as it foams put in the birds, skin side down. Season, and cook slowly for 15-20 minutes until golden-brown. Turn the birds and moisten with half the wine, cover and continue cooking very gently until tender (about 20-30 minutes). Dish up the chicken and keep hot.

Tip the remaining wine into the pan, bring to the boil, scrape the bottom and sides of the pan well and allow to reduce to half the quantity. Mix the arrowroot with half the stock and set aside.

Rub the pâté de foie through a nylon strainer, then mix it with the remaining stock. Thicken the juices in the pan with the slaked arrowroot, bring to the boil and strain into a small pan. Add the pâté mixture and cream. Reheat carefully, taste for seasoning and then spoon sauce over the chicken.

Garnish with watercress and serve with new potatoes and sliced green beans.

Cutting the backbone from the split poussin with poultry scissors

Cutting away the rib-cage after the backbone has been removed

Adding the pâté mixture and cream to the pan for the sauce

Spring chicken alsacienne is served with the sauce spooned over it and is garnished with watercress

Spring chicken bonne femme

4 poussins
4-6 oz belly pork
salt and pepper
2 oz butter
16 small new potatoes (scraped)
$7\frac{1}{2}$ fl oz chicken stock (see page 156)
bouquet garni
12 pickling onions, or shallots
1 dessertspoon arrowroot
2 tablespoons single cream, or top
of the milk
1 tablespoon chopped parsley

Method

Put the pork in pan, cover with water and simmer for 45 minutes, then remove the skin and any small bones and cut into lardons.

Meanwhile season the inside of the poussins and truss them firmly. Melt $1\frac{1}{2}$ oz of the butter in a large stewpan, put in the poussins and potatoes and brown them slowly on all sides. Moisten with 5 tablespoons of stock, tuck in the bouquet garni, cover the pan tightly and cook gently on top of the stove for 20-30 minutes or in the oven, pre-set at 350°F or Mark 4, for 30-35 minutes.

Blanch the onions in a pan of cold water brought to boiling point for 5 minutes, then drain them.

Take up the poussins, remove the trussing strings and keep the birds warm in a deep dish ; lift the potatoes out of the pan with

The poussins and new potatoes are browned in butter, then pot roasted

a draining spoon and keep warm with the chicken. Remove the bouquet garni. Drop the remaining $\frac{1}{2}$ oz butter into the pan and add the pork and onions. Cover and shake the pan occasionally until they are evenly browned and tender. Tip on the remaining stock, bring to the boil and thicken with the arrow-root mixed with the cream.

Return the poussins and potatoes to the pan, sprinkle with chopped parsley and serve with French beans.

Serve the poussins and potatoes in the sauce and sprinkle the whole dish with chopped parsley.

Chicken Khoreshe

2 chickens (each 2 lb), or one 3 lb
   chicken
butter (to sauté)
2-3 large aubergines
2 large onions (sliced)
1 green pepper (shredded and
   blanched)
1 lb tomatoes (skinned, seeds
   removed, and sliced) — see page
   156

salt and pepper
grated rind of $\frac{1}{2}$, and the juice of 1,
   large lemon
oil (to sauté)
good pinch of saffron (soaked in 3
   tablespoons water)

This quantity serves 5-6 people.

Method

Slice aubergines $\frac{1}{4}$ inch thick,
sprinkle with salt and place
them in a colander to drain,
weighted down with a plate.

Set oven at 360°F or Mark 4.
Cut the chickens into neat
joints and brown in butter,
arrange them in a casserole or
deep baking dish in layers with
the onions, pepper and tomatoes ; season, add lemon juice
and rind. Cover tightly and cook
in pre-set oven for about 1 hour.

Meanwhile dry the aubergine
slices and brown quickly in oil.
Pour the saffron liquid over the
ingredients in the casserole,
adding a little jellied stock if
necessary, and place the aubergine slices on top. Return the
dish to the oven, uncovered,
and cook for a further 15
minutes. Serve with new potatoes and French beans or with
a rice pilaf (see page 25).
Note : The onions may be
blanched after slicing.

Chicken
à la suisse

$3\frac{1}{2}$ lb roasting chicken
4 thin rashers of streaky bacon
1 large onion (thinly sliced)
2 large carrots (thinly sliced)
1 stick of celery (sliced)
$2\frac{1}{2}$ fl oz stock (made from chicken
   giblets — see page 156)
bouquet garni
$\frac{1}{2}$ lb noodles
1 oz butter
pepper (ground from mill)
$\frac{1}{2}$ oz Parmesan cheese (grated)

For mornay sauce
1 oz butter
1 oz plain flour
$\frac{3}{4}$ pint flavoured milk
2 oz Emmenthal, or Gruyère,
   cheese (grated)
salt and pepper
2-3 tablespoons double cream

Method

Lay the bacon on the bottom of
a deep pan, cover with the onion,
carrot and celery and set the
trussed chicken on top. Cover
the pan and cook over very
gentle heat for 10-15 minutes.
Pour the stock over the chicken,
tuck in the bouquet garni with
the vegetables, cover again and
cook gently, either on top of
the stove or in the oven, pre-set
at 325-350°F or Mark 3-4, for
about 50-60 minutes.

Meanwhile curl the noodles
into a large pan of boiling salted
water, reduce the heat a little
and boil until just tender ; drain,
refresh and put back into the
rinsed pan with $\frac{1}{2}$ pint hand-hot
water.

Prepare the sauce (see
method, page 151) then beat in
the grated Emmenthal (or
Gruyère) a little at a time and
taste for seasoning. Add the
cream and keep the sauce warm.

Take up the chicken, reduce

the gravy a little and strain. Skim off as much fat as possible, then add the liquid to the cheese sauce. Drain the noodles and heat them in the butter, adding plenty of pepper from the mill before tipping into a hot flame-proof serving dish. Carve the chicken, arrange joints on top of the noodles and coat with the sauce. Dust with the grated Parmesan and brown lightly under the grill.

The noodles for chicken à la suisse are tossed in pepper and butter

Chicken joints on noodles have been coated with sauce before browning

Chicken farci alsacienne

3 ½ lb roasting chicken
1 ½ oz butter
salt and pepper
2 glasses golden sherry
½ pint stock (made from giblets)

For pilaf
5 oz long grain rice
½ lb salt belly pork
bouquet garni
1 oz butter
1 medium-size onion (finely
  chopped)
¾-1 pint stock (made from giblets)
½ bayleaf

For demi-glace sauce
2 tablespoons finely diced onion
1 tablespoon finely diced carrot
1 dessertspoon diced celery
2 tablespoons oil
¾ oz plain flour
1 pint jellied brown bone stock (see
  page 156)
1 teaspoon tomato purée
1 tablespoon chopped mushroom
  peelings
bouquet garni

Method
First cook the salt pork with bouquet garni in enough water to cover for 1 hour; allow to cool a little in the liquid, then remove the skin and bones and chop finely. Make about 1½ pints stock from the chicken giblets (see page 156).

Set the oven at 400°F or Mark 6. Rub the chicken well with the butter, season the inside with salt and pepper and put in a small nut of butter. Set bird in a roasting tin with 1 glass of sherry and ¼ pint of stock and roast in the pre-set moderately hot oven for 1-1¼ hours, basting and turning it from time to time.

Meanwhile prepare the pilaf and sauce. To make the pilaf: melt the butter in a flameproof casserole, add the onion and rice and cook slowly for a few minutes until the rice looks clear. Then add ¾ pint stock and bring to the boil. Stir the prepared pork into the rice with a fork. Add the bayleaf, cover

Poultry scissors are used to cut away the breastbone of chicken after suprêmes have been removed

The suprêmes are sliced and re-placed on the chicken after it has been filled with savoury pilaf

casserole tightly and cook in the oven with the chicken for about 20 minutes. Test to see if the rice is done and add extra stock if necessary.

Prepare the sauce (see method, page 73).

Take up the chicken, cut the suprêmes from each side of the breast and cut away the breastbone. Put the chicken on a serving dish, fill the body with the pilaf, slice the suprêmes and replace them on the bird.

Watchpoint Use just enough pilaf to fill the carcass of the chicken nicely ; serve the rest separately. Deglaze the pan with the reserved stock and second glass of sherry and strain this liquid into the sauce. Simmer until well reduced. Spoon a little of the sauce over the chicken and hand the rest separately. Serve with French beans.

Just before serving, spoon a little sauce over the stuffed chicken

Chicken with red wine and mushrooms

6 chicken joints
little oil (for grilling)
½ cup chicken stock (see page 156)
kneaded butter, or arrowroot
　(to thicken)
½-1 bunch of watercress (to garnish)

For marinade
4-6 oz firm white button mushrooms
2-3 tablespoons olive oil
2 shallots (finely chopped)
2 wineglasses red wine
pepper (ground from mill)
little salt
bouquet garni

Choose 4 breast joints and 2 thigh joints, then you will have enough white meat for 4 people and at the same time can offer a choice of dark meat.

Method
First prepare the marinade : cut the mushrooms in thick slices, mix the other ingredients, reserving the bouquet garni, and add to the mushrooms. Lay the chicken joints in a flat dish and pour the marinade over them, tucking the bouquet garni in the centre. Cover with a lid or foil and leave for 1-2 hours, or longer if preferred, before cooking.

When ready to cook, heat the grill, take the chicken joints from the marinade, brush them with a little oil, and grill for about 6 minutes on each side, allowing a minute or two longer on the skin side to ensure that it gets crisp and golden. Then slide them off the rack into the bottom of the griller pan, spoon over the marinade, removing the bouquet garni, and replace the pan under the grill and continue to cook (for about 10-15 minutes), basting well with the marinade. Lower the heat if necessary after the first 4-5 minutes.

Put the joints on a hot serving dish. Tip the contents of the griller pan into a saucepan, add ½ cup stock, bring to the boil and thicken with a little kneaded butter or slaked arrowroot. Bring to the boil again and spoon sauce over the chicken joints. Garnish with watercress. Serve with sprouts and heated potato crisps.

Left : preparing marinade in which chicken is soaked before cooking
Right : chicken with red wine and mushrooms is served garnished with a bunch of crisp watercress

Chicken Majorca

1 roasting chicken (2½-2¾ lb dressed weight)
2 tablespoons olive oil
½ oz butter
1 medium-size onion (thinly sliced)
1 dessertspoon plain flour
1 wineglass strong stock (made from the giblets — see page 156)
1 wineglass white wine
salt and pepper
bouquet garni (with a strip of orange rind)
1 red pepper
1 large orange
4 large green olives (cut into shreds)
1 tablespoon chopped parsley

Method

Joint the chicken. Heat a large sauté or frying pan and put in the oil, then the butter. When foaming, put in the joints of chicken, skin side down, and sauté until golden-brown. Turn them over and sauté on the other side. Remove the pieces from the pan, add the onion to the pan and allow to colour very slightly. Stir in the flour, add the stock and the wine and bring to the boil. Season, and replace the joints of chicken and the bouquet garni ; cover the pan and simmer either on cooker top, or in moderate oven, pre-set at 350°F or Mark 4, for 20-25 minutes.

Meanwhile grill the pepper, or toast in a flame, until it is charred all over, then remove the skin with a knife ; cut the flesh into shreds and take out the seeds. If necessary, rinse it under the cold tap. Remove rind and the pith from the orange ; slice into rounds. Shred the olives, discarding the stones.

To dish up, take up the chicken joints, trim them and arrange in a hot serving dish. Add the pepper, orange, olives and parsley to the sauce, boil up well and spoon over the dish. Serve with boiled new potatoes and green beans.

Above : putting the sautéd chicken joints back in the pan after the sauce has been made
Below : removing skin and seeds from the red pepper after it has been charred under the grill

Stuffed spring chickens in aspic

(Poussins farçis en gelée)

14 double poussins
1¾ lb veal, or pork (minced)
1 medium-size onion (finely
   chopped)
2 oz butter
1 rounded tablespoon chopped
   thyme and parsley
1 pint measure (6 oz) of fresh white
   breadcrumbs
2 small eggs (beaten)
salt and pepper

To roast
½-¾ lb butter
2 pints strong stock (made from the
   giblets — see page 156)

To garnish
aspic jelly (see page 150)
water cress

These can be made the day before a party and garnished on the day. Store in the refrigerator. This quantity serves 12 people.

Method

Ask your butcher to partially bone out the poussins ; season the cut surface.

Set the oven at 400°F or Mark 6. Soften the onion in the butter, cool, then add it to the minced veal (or pork) with the herbs and crumbs. Mix well, bind with the egg and season well. Divide this farce equally between the poussins, reshape them, sew up and truss. Spread butter thickly on greaseproof paper or foil, tuck this over and round the poussins and pour enough stock into the roasting tin just to cover the bottom. Roast in pre-set oven for 35-40 minutes, basting well and turning the birds over 2 or 3 times ; add more stock to the tin if necessary.

Take up birds, deglaze the tin with stock and pour off into a bowl. Leave to get quite cold. When the poussins are cold also, remove strings, split and trim. Arrange poussins down long serving dishes.

Scoop off the butter from the gravy and spoon the jelly over the chicken. Garnish dish with watercress and 'croûtes' of aspic jelly. Serve with a variety of salads.

Carving turkey

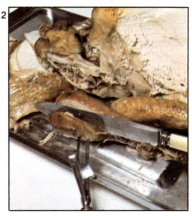

1 Set the bird on the carving dish with the breast towards you. Insert the fork into the carcass between the leg and the breast, then slice the skin between the leg and carcass and bend the leg outwards. Carve the breast in curving slices, starting from the wing and working up to the rib-cage (as shown), and taking in a piece of breast stuffing

2 Separate the drumstick from the thigh joint and then cut thin slices of dark meat from these and serve each person with a portion of this, a slice of breast and some stuffing. When you have completed one side of the bird, turn it round and carve the other side

The method for **French roast** turkey is very similar to chicken (see page 11). For a frozen turkey weighing 12 lb and under, allow 15 minutes per lb and 15 minutes over, in an oven set at 350°F or Mark 4. For a fresh bird, 12 lb and over, allow 10 minutes per lb and 10 minutes over.

Roast stuffed turkey

8 lb turkey (dressed)
3-4 oz butter, or bacon fat (for roasting)
1 pint stock (made from giblets — see chicken stock, page 156)
1 rounded tablespoon plain flour (for gravy)

For stuffing
1 medium-size onion (finely chopped)
2 oz butter
1 lb pork (minced)
1 cup fresh white breadcrumbs
salt and pepper
1 teaspoon dried sage
$\frac{1}{2}$ teaspoon mixed dried herbs
1 tablespoon chopped parsley
2-3 tablespoons stock, or water

Trussing needle and fine string

This quantity serves 8 people.

Method

First prepare stuffing : blanch onion by putting it in pan of cold water and bringing to the boil for 5 minutes ; drain, refresh and return to the pan with butter. Cover pan with buttered paper and lid and cook onion slowly for about 5 minutes until it is golden-brown ; allow to cool.

Mix the pork, breadcrumbs, seasoning and herbs together with a fork, then add the onion. Work in the stock or water a little at a time.

Set oven at 350°F or Mark 4. Stuff the turkey at the neck end (you should also have enough stuffing for the body cavity because if the stuffing bulges out too much it might get dry and overcooked).

Watchpoint Do not stuff the turkey until the day it is to be cooked.

Pull flap of neck skin gently over stuffing and fasten under the wing tips with a skewer. Then truss the bird.

Put turkey into a roasting tin, spread butter or bacon fat over a double sheet of greaseproof paper or sheet of foil ; lay this over the bird and pour round half the stock. French roast in pre-set oven, allowing 15 minutes per lb and 15 minutes over. Turn and baste bird every 20 minutes but keep paper or foil on while cooking.

If stock reduces too much during cooking, add a little more. After 1 hour cut trussing string holding the legs. To test if the bird is cooked pierce thigh with a skewer ; if clear juice runs out, the bird is ready. If bird is not brown enough towards end of cooking time, remove paper and leave bird until golden-brown.

Once cooked, set bird on a serving dish, pull out trussing string and skewers. Keep the turkey warm.

To make gravy : strain juices from roasting tin into a pan and deglaze tin with remaining stock. Add this to juices in pan and skim off some of the fat. Put fat back into tin, stir in flour, then liquid from pan ; stir until boiling. Season and strain gravy back into pan. When ready to serve turkey, reheat gravy and serve it separately.

Turkey mayonnaise

white turkey meat (cut in julienne
   strips, 1½-2 inches long)
1 can consommé (about 10 fl oz)
scant ½ oz gelatine
1 glass sherry

To decorate
3-4 gherkins
1 small jar of green olives
   (stuffed with pimiento)
5 tablespoons stock (see page 156)
   or water
scant ½ oz gelatine
½ pint mayonnaise (see page 151)

*8-9 inch diameter sandwich, or deep
   cake, tin*

This quantity serves 8 people.

Method

Have enough white turkey meat cut in julienne strips to fill a 5-inch diameter basin (not tightly packed). Leave turkey strips on a plate.

Heat the consommé in a pan ; soak first portion of gelatine in the sherry until it has swelled, then add this liquid to the consommé and stir gently until gelatine is dissolved ; allow to cool.

Cut the gherkins in slanting slices and cut a few olives in neat rounds.

Place cake tin in a roasting tin containing 2-3 ice cubes and a little cold water. Pour in a very thin layer of the cold but still liquid consommé and leave to set before arranging your garnish of gherkins and olives in a bold pattern on this.

To do this quickly and well, lift each piece of garnish with a trussing needle (the dedicated cook uses an old fashioned hatpin kept specially for the purpose), dip it into the cold con-sommé and place garnish in position. Now spoon over just enough cold consommé to hold the decoration in position. Put in the refrigerator to set.

Then pour in more cold consommé so that you have a layer about ½ inch deep, return the tin to the refrigerator or cold larder to set.

Soak the remaining gelatine in the stock or water for about 1 minute, then dissolve it in a pan over gentle heat ; then add to the mayonnaise. Pour the mayonnaise over the turkey meat and mix together carefully ; spoon this into the prepared tin, cover with foil and leave to set.

To serve : dip the bottom of the tin very quickly in and out of a bowl of very hot water to loosen the turkey mayonnaise ; ease it away from the sides very quickly with a palette or round-bladed knife.

Place the serving dish over the top of the tin, hold firmly and turn over ; lift off the tin. (If the tin doesn't lift off the first time, shake it and the dish gently from side to side — not up and down which would spoil the shape.)

Roast turkey with oyster stuffing

1 hen turkey (weighing 8-12 lb)
giblets
root vegetables (diced)
salt and pepper
arrowroot, or cornflour (slaked)
—to thicken
little gravy browning (optional)
2 oz butter (softened) — for
roasting

For oyster stuffing
2 cans (6 oz each) of oysters
1 large onion (finely chopped)
6 oz butter
3 cups fresh white breadcrumbs
3 sticks of celery (chopped)
1 teaspoon mixed dried herbs
1 tablespoon chopped parsley
little milk, or water (to bind)

Trussing needle and fine string, or
*   poultry pins*

This quantity serves 8-10 people.

1 *Mixing together browned onion,*
breadcrumbs and celery for stuffing,
before adding the chopped oysters
2 *Wrapping foil round the turkey*

Method

First prepare the stock for the gravy : put the giblets, root vegetables and seasoning in a large pan with water to cover and simmer for 1-2 hours ; strain and keep stock aside for the gravy. Thicken it with a little slaked arrowroot or cornflour and colour it, if necessary, with a little of your favourite gravy browning.

Set oven at 325°F or Mark 3.

To prepare oyster stuffing ; cook the onion in butter until it is golden-coloured, add about one-third of the breadcrumbs and stir over heat until the butter is absorbed. Tip mixture into a bowl, add the remaining crumbs, celery, herbs and seasoning. Drain, rinse and drain the oysters ; lightly chop them, add to the mixture and bind with a little milk or water. Wipe out the cavity of the turkey with a damp cloth and rub the inside with $\frac{1}{2}$ teaspoon salt. Put in the stuffing, sew up with fine string and a trussing needle, or secure with poultry pins and string. Rub turkey with the

softened butter and wrap in foil. Cook in pre-set oven for 4-4$\frac{1}{2}$ hours, unwrapping the foil and increasing the heat to 400°F or Mark 6 for the last 20 minutes of cooking time.

Serve turkey with roast potatoes, cooked in a separate pan, and broccoli spears plainly boiled and finished with a little butter. Reheat and serve the gravy separately.

Turkey en gelée

10-12 lb turkey
1 medium-size onion (peeled and stuck with a clove)
3 oz butter
$\frac{1}{4}$ pint stock (see chicken stock page 156)
1 glass sherry

For mousse
1$\frac{1}{2}$ lb cooked ham
$\frac{1}{2}$ lb butter (creamed)
$\frac{1}{2}$ pint béchamel sauce (made with 1$\frac{1}{2}$ oz butter, 1$\frac{1}{2}$ oz plain flour and $\frac{1}{2}$ pint flavoured milk)
$\frac{1}{4}$ pint double cream
$\frac{1}{2}$ lb cooked tongue (finely shredded)
salt and pepper

For garnish
2 pints aspic jelly (see page 150)
8 oz quantity of rich shortcrust pastry (see page 153)
1 truffle
2 cans cranberry sauce

16 small tartlet tins

This quantity serves 8-10 people.

Method

Set the oven at 375°F or Mark 5. Place the onion and 1 oz of the butter inside the bird, place in a roasting tin and pour round the stock and sherry. Melt the remaining butter and pour it over the turkey. Cover the bird with greaseproof paper and foil and French roast in the pre-set oven, allowing 15 minutes to the pound and 15 minutes over. Leave the turkey to cool.

Prepare the aspic jelly. Make the shortcrust pastry and set aside to chill. Line the pastry on to the small tartlet tins and bake blind (for about 8 minutes in an oven pre-set at 375°F or Mark 5). Allow to cool.

To prepare the mousse : pass the ham through the mincer twice and then mix with the creamed butter and cold béchamel sauce. Partially whip the cream and fold it into the ham mixture with the tongue and season well.

Cut the wing and breast fillets, each in one piece, from the turkey and remove the breast-

Shaping the mousse on the carcass to simulate the breastbone of turkey

Basting the turkey with aspic after arranging the sliced suprêmes on it

bone with poultry scissors. Fill
the carcass with the mousse,
shaping it carefully with a
palette knife to simulate the
shape of the breastbone.
Carve each fillet in neat, even-
size slices and replace on the
mousse. Arrange slices of truffle
along line of removed breastbone. Baste with cold aspic
jelly and leave to set.

Chop the remaining aspic,
place on a large serving dish
and set the turkey on top. Fill
each tartlet case with a spoonful of cranberry sauce and
arrange round the turkey.

*The turkey en gelée is served with
tartlets filled with cranberry sauce*

Galantine of turkey

12 lb turkey
3-4 tablespoons salad oil
2 glasses sherry
½ pint jellied stock (see page 156)

For stuffing
6 oz butter
2 onions (finely chopped)
2 lb cooked ham (shoulder cut)
— minced
1 lb raw veal (minced)
12 oz fresh white breadcrumbs
1 tablespoon mixed chopped herbs
grated rind and juice of 2 oranges
salt and pepper
1 egg (beaten)

For serving
1 quart aspic jelly (see page 150)
bouquets of watercress

Trussing needle and fine string

This quantity serves 8-10 people.

Method

Ask the butcher to bone out your turkey.

To prepare stuffing: melt butter, add onion, cook until it is soft but not coloured and allow to cool. Mix ham, veal, breadcrumbs and herbs together and add to onion. Add orange rind and juice, season and bind mixture with beaten egg.

Spread stuffing over turkey, roll it up and sew with fine string, then tie at intervals along galantine to keep stuffing in position. Set oven at 350°F or Mark 4.

Heat oil in a roasting tin, add galantine, pour over sherry and stock and baste well. Cover with a piece of buttered paper or foil and French roast for 3-3 ½ hours in pre-set moderate oven, reducing heat to 325°F or Mark 3 for the last hour when galantine will be well coloured. Turn and baste it every 20 minutes throughout the cooking, adding extra stock, if necessary, to keep it moist. Remove galantine from tin and allow it to cool. Then wrap in foil and keep in refrigerator before finishing the next day.

To finish galantine: after removing string, brush it with cool aspic, on the point of setting. Cut meat in even slices and arrange these on a large serving dish; baste them with cool, but still liquid, aspic and allow to set. Garnish dish with watercress, and serve with a variety of salads.

Duck and goose

The rich, succulent duck is less versatile than chicken but just as rewarding.
Try the traditional English and French recipes, or make food fit for the gods, with a rich honey roast.

An old goose should be kept in the farmyard, but a young green goose, or gosling, stuffed and roasted, is a table delicacy that has been prized for centuries.

Preparation

Though they are available all year round, duck and ducklings are at their best in the early summer, goose around Christmas. They don't serve as many as a chicken of similar weight, as they're shallow-breasted. A 4 lb duck (plucked weight) is only enough for four people.

Roast birds in a hot oven at 375°F or Mark 5, or on a spit. A little butter or dripping may be spread on the breast but, if bird is a good plump one, it can be put in the oven dry.

Once the fat begins to run, baste bird well and turn it over about every 20 minutes so that skin can brown and crisp. The gravy can be lightly thickened.

Roasting times are 15 minutes per lb and 15 minutes over.

Classic accompaniments to roast duck are sage and onion stuffing, apple sauce, peas and new potatoes ; for goose, apple or gooseberry sauce.

Carving cooked duck/goose
Since these birds are awkward to carve, this is best done in the kitchen.

Small or medium-size bird
(see below)
Remove trussing strings and set the bird on a board.

Cut straight down through breastbone and back. Use scissors to cut through bone.

Lay each half on board, make a slanting cut between ribs to separate wing and leg, making two good portions of each half. With scissors, trim away any carcass bone. The portions should be two wings and two legs, with a piece of breast on all portions. (See page 82 for jointing a raw duck).

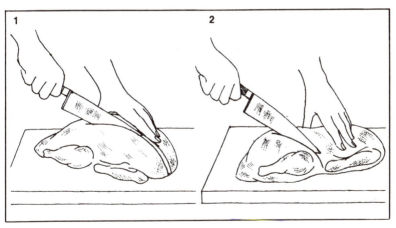

1 *First set bird on a board and cut down through the breastbone and back. Scissors are best for cutting through bone ; use knife for flesh*

2 *Lay each half on the board and make a slanting cut between ribs to separate the wing and leg ; this gives four portions. Trim away bone*

Preparation continued

Large bird

Cut off legs. Remember that leg joint is set differently to a chicken, right under back of the bird.

Raise fillets (wing and breast) by slipping knife under them and along carcass down to wing bones which can then be severed at joint. Slice off a piece of breast with each wing bone attached.

Cut rest of the breast into slanting slices.

To serve : arrange legs at one end of a hot serving dish, wings at other end, pieces of breast in centre. Pour on gravy or sauce.

1 Set bird on a board, then cut off the legs

2 Take a knife and slip it under fillets (wings and breast) to raise them, then slide it along carcass down to wing bones, which can be severed

3 Make the first cut along the breastbone, then make parallel cuts to it down breast, taking care that knife is well slanted towards the inside

4 To loosen the slices, return your knife along the first cut and then cut upwards towards the breastbone. This will give good-looking, long slices

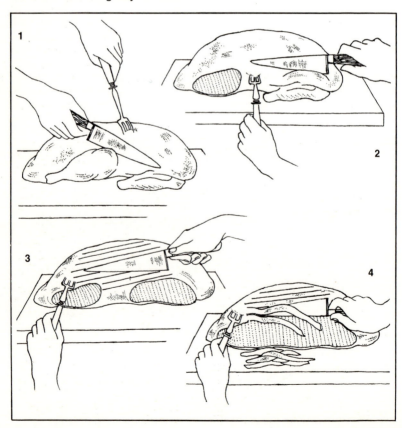

Duck with turnips (aux navets)

4 lb duckling
$1\frac{1}{2}$ oz butter
1 lemon
salt and pepper
$\frac{1}{4}$ pint stock (see chicken stock, page 156)
$\frac{1}{2}$ pint demi-glace sauce (see page 73)
1 wineglass white wine
For garnish
1 lb small new turnips
1 oz butter
1 tablespoon caster sugar
$\frac{1}{2}$ lb small onions (blanched)

This recipe should only be made with small, new turnips. Do not attempt it with the large, old variety as they are much too strong in flavour.

Method

Set oven at 400°F or Mark 6. Place the thinly-pared rind of of the lemon inside the bird with a good nut of butter and seasoning. Smear remaining butter over the breast ; truss the bird and place it in a roasting tin with the stock. Roast it in pre-set oven, basting and turning from time to time.

Meanwhile prepare the demi-glace sauce . Blanch the turnips, melt the butter and place in a shallow pan or casserole with the caster sugar. Cook over a gentle heat, shaking the pan from time to time, until turnips are tender and the sugar has caramelised. Then add the blanched onions and cook for a few more minutes.

Remove the duck from pan and keep hot on a serving dish, skim off fat, add the wine, and the juice of $\frac{1}{2}$ lemon to the roasting tin and boil well. Strain this mixture into the demi-glace sauce, reduce rapidly until syrupy. Spoon a little sauce over the duck (serve the remainder separately), garnish with turnips and onions.

Roast duck Hymettus

1 large duck (about 5 lb dressed
   weight)
giblets
1 teaspoon oil
salt
1 onion (not peeled)
$\frac{1}{2}$ oz butter
2 tablespoons clear honey
juice of $\frac{1}{2}$ lemon
1 tablespoon arrowroot (slaked
   with 2 tablespoons water)

For stuffing
1 oz butter
1 medium-size onion (chopped)
4 oz walnut kernels, or cashew
   nuts (chopped)
4 oz fresh white breadcrumbs
grated rind of 1 lemon
1 tablespoon chopped parsley
1 teaspoon chopped sage
1 teaspoon chopped thyme, or
   marjoram
$\frac{1}{2}$ teaspoon cinnamon
salt and pepper
1 egg (beaten)
juice of $\frac{1}{2}$ lemon

For garnish
$\frac{1}{2}$ bunch of watercress
1 lemon (sliced)

Method

Brown the giblets, but not the liver, in 1 teaspoon oil, cover with 1 pint cold water, bring to the boil and skim well. Season with salt and 1 onion (washed and trimmed but not peeled) and simmer gently for 30-45 minutes. Strain to make stock. Set oven at 375°F or Mark 5.

To prepare the stuffing : melt half the butter, add the onion and cook slowly until soft but not coloured, drop the remaining butter into the pan and, when melted, add the nuts and fry until golden-brown. Turn the nuts and onions into a bowl, add the rest of the ingredients and mix well. Stuff into the body of the duck and truss neatly.

Rub the $\frac{1}{2}$ oz butter over the duck and then spread with the honey. Roast in pre-set oven for $1\frac{1}{2}$ hours (15 minutes per lb and 15 minutes over), basting and turning from time to time.

Take up the duck, remove the trussing strings, trim the leg and wing joints and set on the serving dish.

Tip off the fat, leaving any sediment at the bottom of the pan, add the strained lemon juice and stock. Bring to the boil, season well and thicken with the arrowroot.

Garnish the duck with watercress and lemon slices, and serve with the gravy in a sauce boat.

Note : new potatoes, boiled and tossed in a little butter and chopped parsley, are best with duck. For a vegetable, serve frozen sliced green beans (for preparation, see right).

Mixing breadcrumbs with onions and nuts to make stuffing for duck

Adding beans to bacon and onion before tossing them over the heat for haricots verts béarnais

Haricots verts béarnais

1 lb packet of sliced, or whole, frozen French (haricot) beans
4 rashers of back bacon
½ oz butter
1 medium-size onion (finely chopped)
black pepper (ground from mill)

Method

Cook the beans following the instructions on the packet ; drain and refresh them with cold water. Drain well. Remove the rind and rust from the bacon and cut into ½-inch strips, set aside. Melt the butter in a sauté pan, add the onion and cook slowly until soft but not coloured, then add the bacon to the pan, increase the heat and fry until the bacon is crisp and the onion brown. Tip the beans into the pan and toss until hot, adding black pepper from the mill.

Spreading honey over buttered duck, stuffed and trussed ready to cook

Trimming leg and wing joints with poultry scissors for serving

Roast duck Hymettus continued

Ready to serve : roast duck Hymettus is accompanied by haricots verts

Duck with orange

4 lb duck
3 oranges
1½ oz butter
salt and pepper
¼ pint stock (see page 155)
1 wineglass red wine
1-2 tablespoons redcurrant
   jelly (see page 154)
watercress (to garnish)

For ½ pint demi-glace sauce
3 tablespoons oil
1 small onion (finely diced)
1 small carrot (finely diced)
½ stick of celery (finely diced)
1 rounded tablespoon plain flour
1 pint well-flavoured brown
   stock
1 teaspoon tomato purée
1 tablespoon mushroom peelings
   (chopped), or 1 mushroom
bouquet garni

Method

Set the oven at 400°F or Mark 6. Place the thinly pared rind of 1 orange inside the duck with a good nut of butter and seasoning. Spread remaining butter over the breast. Truss the bird and place it in a roasting tin with the stock. Roast in pre-set oven for 15 minutes per lb and 15 minutes over, basting and turning the bird from time to time.

Meanwhile, prepare the oranges for the garnish. Cut them into segments, removing all the pith and membranes. Reserve any juice.

To prepare demi-glace sauce : heat a small pan, put in the oil, add the diced vegetables. Cook together on a low heat until the vegetables are barely coloured. Stir in the flour and cook slowly, stirring occasionally, until it is russet-brown. Draw pan aside, cool mixture a little, and add ¾ pint of cold stock and the remaining ingredients. Season and bring sauce to the boil, half cover the pan and cook sauce gently for 35-40 minutes, skimming it when necessary.

Add half the remaining stock to the pan, bring it to the boil and skim ; simmer for 5 minutes. Repeat this process with remaining stock, then strain sauce, return it to a clean pan and cook until syrupy.

Remove the duck from the roasting tin and keep hot on a serving dish. Tip off the fat from the roasting tin, leave the sediment behind, then add wine and reserved orange juice ; boil up well. Strain into demi-glace sauce, add redcurrant jelly and simmer until it is a syrupy consistency. Adjust seasoning.

Spoon a little sauce over the duck, garnish it with watercress at one end and with orange segments at the other. Serve the remaining sauce separately.

Braised duckling with olives

1 duckling
1 oz butter
1 medium-size onion (sliced)
1 glass port
1 teaspoon paprika pepper
$\frac{1}{2}$ pint jellied stock (see page 155)
bouquet garni
salt and pepper
2 tomatoes
12 large green olives, or olives
    stuffed with pimiento
1 dessertspoon plain flour

Method

Brown the duck in the butter in a deep casserole ; when evenly coloured, tip off the fat and add the onion ; cover and cook slowly until the onion is soft.

Moisten bird with the port ; allow liquid to reduce by half and then stir in the paprika and cook for 2-3 minutes. Pour on the stock, add the bouquet garni and season lightly. Cover casserole and cook very gently for about 45 minutes or until duckling is tender. This cooking can be done on top of the stove, or in the oven pre-set at 350°F or Mark 4.

Meanwhile skin and quarter the tomatoes (see page 156) remove the seeds, then cut the flesh again into neat shreds. Set aside.

If using large olives, cut in strips off the stones ; if using stuffed olives, leave them whole, blanch in boiling water for 5 minutes, drain and leave to soak in cold water for 30 minutes, then drain again.

Remove the duckling from the casserole and keep hot ; take out the bouquet garni. Skim the fat from the liquid in casserole. Mix the flour with 1 tablespoon of the liquid, return this to the casserole and stir until it boils.

Cook liquid for 5 minutes. Add the tomatoes and olives, reheat and taste for seasoning.

Divide the duckling into four

portions, place them in a hot
serving dish and spoon over the
sauce. Serve with beans, peas
and very tiny roast potatoes.

*The cooked duckling ready to serve,
shown with the raw ingredients*

Ballotine of duck

1 duck (weighing 3-4 lb)
2 tablespoons cooking oil
1 glass dry sherry
$\frac{1}{4}$ lb button mushrooms (sliced)
$\frac{1}{2}$ oz butter
watercress (to garnish)

For stuffing
1 oz butter
1 onion (finely chopped)
12 oz pork, or veal (minced)
1 teacup fresh white breadcrumbs
1 dessertspoon chopped parsley
1 teaspoon dried sage
1 glass dry sherry
3 oz ham (shredded)
8 pistachio nuts (blanched and
   shredded)
1 egg (beaten)
salt and pepper

For demi-glace sauce
2 tablespoons cooking oil
1 tablespoon finely diced carrot
1 tablespoon finely diced onion
$\frac{1}{2}$ tablespoon finely diced celery
1 rounded tablespoon plain flour
$\frac{3}{4}$ pint stock (see page 155)
few mushroom stalks, or peelings
1 teaspoon tomato purée
salt and pepper
bouquet garni

Trussing needle ; thread, or fine string

Method
Bone out the duck as for a chicken (see page 13). Set the oven at 400°F or Mark 6.

To prepare the stuffing : melt the butter in a pan, add the onion and cook until soft but not coloured. Add to the minced meat and breadcrumbs and mix well with herbs, sherry, ham and pistachios. Bind with the beaten egg and season. Stuff the duck, sew up neatly with fine string and tie at intervals of 1-2 inches.

Heat 2 tablespoons oil in a roasting tin, set the duck on a grid in the tin and baste with the hot oil. Roast in pre-set oven for 1-1$\frac{1}{4}$ hours, Baste every 20 minutes and turn the bird after 40 minutes.

Prepare the sauce (see method, page 73).

Cook the button mushrooms in the $\frac{1}{2}$ oz butter until soft. Take up duck, pour off fat and deglaze the roasting tin with the sherry. Strain and add to the sauce with the cooked mushrooms.

Serve the duck whole or sliced, pour over a little of the sauce and serve the rest of it separately. Garnish with watercress.

As duck is quite a rich meat, choose boiled potatoes (preferably new ones) as an accompanying vegetable. Braised celery is a good second vegetable.

Serve ballotine of duck whole or sliced, with a little sauce spooned over

Salmis of duck

1 duckling
1 oz butter
1 shallot (finely chopped)
¾ oz plain flour
¼ pint chicken, stock (see page 156)
1 wineglass dry white wine
salt and pepper
1 bouquet garni

For garnish
8-10 green olives (stoned)
8-10 chipolata sausages
6-8 croûtes of bread (fried in butter)

Salmis is the name given to a brown ragoût of duck or game. The bird is lightly roasted before being split, jointed or carved and then put in a rich brown sauce flavoured with wine. Further cooking is then done either on top of the stove or in the oven, and the finished dish is garnished with croûtes of bread.

Method

Set oven at 425°F or Mark 7.

Prick the skin of the duckling all over with a trussing needle (this is to help the fat to run), place in a roasting tin and cook in the pre-set hot oven for 30 minutes. Meanwhile, melt the butter in a large pan, add the shallot and cook gently for 1-2 minutes, then blend in the flour and allow it to colour slowly until it is a good russet-brown. Remove pan from the heat, whisk in ½ pint of stock and the wine, return pan to the heat and stir until boiling. Season, add bouquet garni and simmer for 20 minutes.

Tip half the remaining cold stock into the pan, bring to the boil and then skim sauce well. Repeat this process and continue simmering it gently while the duckling is roasting. Take up the duck, joint it and set portions in a shallow ovenproof casserole; spoon over the sauce and cover with a lid. Turn

Carving roast duckling in portions

Adding croûtes of bread to salmis

the oven to 350°F or Mark 4, put in the duck and continue cooking for about 20 minutes.

To prepare garnish; leave the olives to soak in hot water; grill or fry the sausages. For serving, remove the lid of the casserole, garnish the duck with the sausages and drained olives and arrange the fried croûtes around. Serve with new potatoes and minted peas.

Sauté of duck with Burgundy

2 medium-size ducks, or ducklings
1 tablespoon oil or $\frac{1}{2}$ oz butter
1 medium-size onion (finely sliced)
scant oz butter (optional)
6-8 oz button mushrooms
2 wineglasses red Burgundy
   (preferably Mâcon)
1 wineglass jellied stock (see page
   155)
salt and pepper
kneaded butter
fried croûtes of bread (to garnish)
   — optional

This recipe is also good to use for wild duck.

Method

Quickly brown the ducks all over in the oil (or the $\frac{1}{2}$ oz butter) in a large pan (they may have to be done one at a time).

Note : the reason for browning the ducks is to extract some of the fat, as otherwise the sauce would be too greasy. Butter can be used in place of the oil, if preferred, from the point of view of flavour.

Remove birds from the pan and leave to cool a little. Then divide them into four, first cutting down through the breastbone with scissors and then on either side of the backbone through the rib cage ; cut each half into two just above the leg, and set aside. (The backbones can then be used for stock for a stew.) Add the onion to the pan, in which there should be about 1-2 tablespoons of the duck fat (if preferred, use the scant oz of butter). Allow the onion to brown slightly, then add the mushrooms, whole or sliced according to size, and sauté briskly for 2-3 minutes.

Heat the wine in a small pan, reduce it and then add to the pan with the stock. Stir until it boils, season, put in the pieces of duck, cover and simmer for 10 minutes. The duck should be kept slightly pink.

When ready to serve, trim the joints with scissors, if necessary, to remove any ugly bones. Pile meat up in a serving dish, thicken the sauce slightly with kneaded butter, reboil and spoon over the dish.

Note : as with most sautés, there should be just enough sauce to coat the dish nicely and to allow about 2 tablespoons extra for each guest.

This dish may be garnished with fried croûtes of bread. Serve with Sicilian potatoes and brussels sprouts (if possible, the small 'red' home-grown variety).

Sicilian potatoes

$\frac{1}{2}\frac{3}{4}$ lb potatoes (3-4 medium-
   size ones)
1 small orange (preferably a
   blood orange)
pinch of bicarbonate of soda
4 oz butter
2 shallots (finely chopped)
salt and pepper
1 egg yolk (optional)

Method

First put the orange in a pan of water with a pinch of bicarbonate of soda and boil for 45-50 minutes. Peel the potatoes, then boil, drain and dry well and crush with a potato masher or push through a sieve. Turn them into a basin.

Meanwhile set the oven at 400°F or Mark 6. Drain the orange, cut in four and remove any pips then finely chop the quarters (including peel). Melt

2 oz of the butter in a small saucepan, add the shallot and cook until coloured ; cook for 1-2 minutes more, then add the chopped orange. Cook onion mixture, without the lid, until turning colour. Then turn into the sieved potato ; mix with a fork, season well, add 1 oz butter and the egg yolk, if wished.

Melt the remainder of the butter, brush two baking sheets with it, then shape the mixture into large 'marbles'. Put these down the baking sheet at inter-vals and, with the prongs of a fork, flatten each marble to about $\frac{1}{4}$ inch thick. Bake in the pre-set hot oven for about 10-15 minutes or until well browned. Take the baking sheets out of the oven, slip a palette knife under each potato 'cake' and serve them overlapping on a hot dish, with the underside upper-most.

Note : the underside of the potatoes should be brown and practically caramelised so that these cakes are almost crisp.

Sauté of duck with mushrooms

1 duck (3-4 lb) — with its liver
½ pint demi-glace sauce
(see page 73)
1 glass Madeira, or brown sherry
1-2 oz butter
1½-2 fl oz brandy
1 small onion (finely chopped)
salt and pepper

For garnish
4-6 oz even-size mushrooms
1 shallot, or ½ small onion (finely
chopped)
1-2 oz butter
2 tablespoons fresh white breadcrumbs
1 dessertspoon fresh, or 1 teaspoon
dried, chopped herbs
1 tablespoon grated Parmesan
cheese

1 *Cutting the duck into large pieces*
2 *Stuffing mushrooms for garnish*

Method

First prepare the demi-glace sauce. After straining the sauce, add the Madeira (or brown sherry) and continue to simmer for 5-6 minutes ; set aside. Sauté the duck liver lightly, then cool and slice. Put sliced liver into the sauce.

Cut the duck into six neat joints. Sauté these joints in a very little butter. When they are browned, flame with the brandy, and after 1-2 minutes add onion

and seasoning, then cover and simmer for about 20 minutes.

To prepare the garnish : peel and stalk the mushrooms, chop the trimmings finely and add to the shallot. Melt a little butter and toss the shallot and mushroom mixture in it, then add the breadcrumbs and herbs. Remove from pan and set aside. Sauté the mushrooms lightly in the same pan, take out and fill each one with the stuffing mixture, doming the tops. Sprinkle with Parmesan cheese and brown them under the grill or in the oven, set at 425°F or Mark 7, for 4-5 minutes.

Put the duck on to a serving dish and keep hot ; reduce the liquid in the pan and strain into the demi-glace sauce. Reheat this carefully and spoon a little over the duck. Garnish with the mushrooms ; serve the rest of the sauce separately and accompany the dish with peas and small new potatoes.

Roast stuffed goose

1 young goose (about 8 lb)
1 oz butter
½ teaspoon salt
¼ teaspoon pepper
¼ teaspoon ground ginger
1 glass port
½ pint stock (made from goose
   giblets — see method page 156)

For potato stuffing
3 medium-size onions (finely
   chopped)
1½ lb potatoes
4 oz butter, or double cream
1½ teaspoons dried sage
salt and pepper

For garnish
2 oz butter
10 small sharp dessert apples
   (peeled and cored)
4 tablespoons redcurrant jelly (see
   page 154)
2 tablespoons red wine vinegar

This quantity serves 6-8 people.

1 *Filling the body of the goose
with potato stuffing before trussing*
2 *Spreading the breast of the goose
with seasoned butter*

Method

First prepare the stuffing. Cover
the onions with cold water, cook
until tender and drain well. Boil
the potatoes, drain and dry
thoroughly over gentle heat and
mash with a fork ; work in the
butter (or cream), onions and
sage and season well.

Set the oven at 375°F or
Mark 5. Fill the body of the
goose with stuffing, truss, and
sew firmly at each end. Mix
the butter with the seasoning
and ginger and spread over the
breast of the bird. Set in a
roasting tin and cook in the pre-
set moderate oven for about $2\frac{1}{2}$
hours, basting and turning from
time to time. After two hours, tip
off all the fat in the roasting tin,
pour the port over the goose and
continue cooking until the skin
is crisp.

Meanwhile prepare the
garnish. Melt the butter in a
small roasting tin or shallow
ovenproof dish. Put in the
apples, baste them well with the
butter and cook in the oven until
golden-brown (about 40 minutes).

1

2

Put the redcurrant jelly in a pan with the vinegar and melt over heat.

Take up the goose, remove the trussing strings and wing pinions, set on a hot serving dish and surround with the apples. Spoon the melted jelly over the apples.

Skim any fat from the juices in the roasting tin, add the stock and boil up well. Adjust the seasoning ; thicken, if necessary, with a dessertspoon of cornflour and strain into a sauce boat. Serve with château potatoes (see page 153) and brussels sprouts.

Yorkshire pie

1 small plump goose (about 5-6 lb)
1 pheasant, or chicken (about
  2-2½ lb)
1 calf's tongue (about ¾ lb)
1 lb quantity of flaky pastry or 1½ lb
  quantity of shortcrust pastry for
  raised pies (see pages 152, 153)
salt
pepper (ground from mill)
little butter
egg wash (1 egg beaten with pinch
  of salt)
root vegetables and herbs (for stock)

For farce
1 small onion (finely chopped)
¾ oz butter
1½ lb minced pork
4 oz fresh white breadcrumbs
1 dessertspoon mixed dried herbs
1 tablespoon chopped parsley
1 egg (beaten)
little ground mace, or allspice
  (ground from mill)

*15½-inch diameter pie dish, or 10-12
inch diameter raised pie mould, or
deep cake tin with removable base*

This pie can be made in a pie
dish and covered with flaky
pastry, or made as a raised pie.
The former is the simpler way
as really large raised pie moulds
are not easy to find now,
although a deep cake tin can
be substituted. The pie is usually
served cold. This quantity serves
8-10 people.

Method

First soak the tongue in cold
water for 2-3 hours. Then rinse,
cover with cold water and
simmer until tender (about 1½
hours). When cooked, nick the
skin on the underside of the
tongue and peel off carefully.
Pull out the little bones in the
root of the tongue and trim away
some of the fat.

Meanwhile, bone out the birds.
Be careful not to split the skin
as the birds should remain whole.
Reserve the bones for stock.
Season the inside of each bird,
then place the tongue inside the
pheasant (or chicken) and place
that inside the goose. Rub the
surface of goose with a little
butter and season ; roll up.

Set oven at 400°F or Mark 6.
To prepare the farce : soften the
onion in the butter, then mix
with the pork, crumbs and herbs.
Bind with the egg and season

1 *Placing cooked tongue inside the
pheasant for Yorkshire pie*
2 *Putting pheasant inside the goose,
which is then rolled up*

well, adding a little ground mace or allspice.

Roll out the pastry. If making a raised pie, line bottom and sides of the mould, or cake tin, making 'wall' $\frac{1}{2}$-$\frac{3}{4}$ inch thick.

Line bottom and sides of the empty pie dish, or pastry-lined mould, with the farce, keeping back a little for the top. Put the goose in the centre and cover with a thin layer of remaining farce. Cover the pie with pastry, making a small hole in the centre ; trim, and decorate to taste. Brush with egg wash and place pie in centre of the pre-set oven. Bake for 40-50 minutes, or until nicely brown. Then cover pie with a double sheet of wet greaseproof paper, lower the heat to 350°F or Mark 4 and continue to cook for a further $1\frac{1}{2}$-2 hours.

Meanwhile make a strong stock from the bones, with root vegetables and herbs to flavour (see method, page 155). **Watchpoint** If making a raised pie, cool it well before attempting to remove from mould or cake tin.

When pie is quite cold, fill up with the stock, which should now be jellied. If stock has not jellied, add about 1 rounded teaspoon gelatine to every $\frac{1}{4}$ pint of liquid.

Christmas stuffed goose

1 plump goose (about 6-7 lb)
1 roasting chicken (about $2\frac{1}{2}$ lb)
  dressed weight)
1 small game bird (young tender
  pigeon, or squab)
knob of butter (mixed with salt and
  allspice)
plain flour (for dredging)
melted butter (for roasting)

For farce
$1\frac{1}{2}$ lb pork sausage meat
8 oz cooked ham (minced)
livers of the birds (minced)
3 shallots (finely chopped)
6 oz flat mushrooms (washed,
  lightly squeezed and chopped)
4 oz fresh white breadcrumbs
1 tablespoon freshly chopped sage,
  or 1 teaspoon dried sage
pinch of allspice (ground from mill)
pepper (ground from mill)
1-2 beaten eggs (to bind)

For gravy
about 1 dessertspoon plain flour
$\frac{1}{2}$ pint strong stock (made from bones
  of birds, with vegetables and herbs
  to flavour — see page 155)
1-2 tablespoons mushroom ketchup
juice of $\frac{1}{2}$ lemon
good dash of Tabasco sauce, or
  pinch of cayenne pepper

Method
First bone out the birds and make the stock.

Set oven at 400°F or Mark 6. Lay the birds flat on a board or table. Spread the cut surface with the seasoned butter.

Now prepare the farce by mixing the sausage meat, ham, minced livers, shallot, mushrooms, crumbs and herbs together. Season well with allspice and pepper and bind with the egg. Spread this farce on to the cut surface of the birds, lay the chicken skin side down on top of the cut side of goose, then the pigeon on the chicken in the same way.

Roll the goose round the two birds and sew up the joint securely with fine string. Shape into a roly-poly, set the stuffed goose in a roasting tin, dredge lightly with flour and baste it well with melted butter. Put to roast in the pre-set hot oven, basting well with the fat as it runs from the goose. Allow $1\frac{1}{2}$-$1\frac{3}{4}$ hours roasting and once the goose is brown lower the heat to 375°F or Mark 5.

Watchpoint Be careful when roasting the goose that the juices in the tin do not become overbrowned and scorched as this will spoil the flavour of the gravy. If this seems likely to happen, add a little stock.

When the goose is well browned, take up carefully, remove string and set in a serving dish.

To prepare the gravy : pour off as much of the fat from the tin as possible, then add the flour, scraping round the tin well with a metal spoon. Pour in the stock and add the ketchup, lemon juice and Tabasco (or cayenne). Stir well and bring to the boil. Test for seasoning and strain. Pour a little of the gravy round the goose and serve the rest separately.

Braised goose (or capon)

1 young, tender ('green') goose, or capon (about 5-6 lb)

For farce
1 lb minced pork, or sausage meat
1 cup fresh white breadcrumbs
1 dessertspoon dried herbs
1 tablespoon fresh chopped parsley
1 medium-size onion
1 oz butter
salt and pepper
pinch of ground mace
1 egg (beaten)

For braising
little dripping, or butter
2 onions (sliced)
2 carrots (sliced)
1 turnip (diced)
2-3 sticks of celery (sliced)
bouquet garni
6 peppercorns
$\frac{3}{4}$-1 pint good brown stock (see page 155)
1 wineglass red wine

For brown sauce
1 tablespoon each finely diced carrot and onion
1 stick of celery (diced)
1-2 tablespoons dripping
1 tablespoon plain flour
1 teaspoon tomato purée
$\frac{1}{2}$-$\frac{3}{4}$ pint stock (see page 155)
2 wineglasses red wine
little slaked arrowroot (optional)

For garnish
braised chestnuts (see page 90)
$\frac{1}{2}$-$\frac{3}{4}$ lb chipolata sausages (fried)

Method
Set oven at 350-375°F or Mark 4-5.

To make the farce ; mix the meat, crumbs and herbs together in a basin. Chop the onion and cook in a pan with the butter until soft, then add to the mixture. Season well, add mace and bind with the egg.

Stuff the goose with farce and truss. Rub a braising pan, or flameproof casserole, with a little dripping or butter. Put the braising vegetables in this, cover and sweat for 5-7 minutes. Then put the goose on top and the bouquet garni and peppercorns at the side. Add the stock. Raise the heat and allow the liquid to reduce by about a quarter, then add the wine ; cover the bird with a piece of paper and then the lid and cook gently in the pre-set oven for about 2 hours, basting frequently. After about $1\frac{1}{2}$ hours, remove the lid and continue to cook, basting well and adding a little more stock if necessary, until the goose is nicely crisp.

Meanwhile prepare the brown sauce by cooking the diced vegetables in 1-2 tablespoons of dripping. When barely coloured, stir in the flour and continue to cook to a russet-brown. Then draw aside and add the tomato purée and stock. Bring to the boil and simmer, with the pan half covered, for about 30 minutes. Then add the wine and continue to cook uncovered for a further 20 minutes. Strain, rinse out the pan and return the sauce to it ; set aside.

Take up the goose, place it on a large meat dish and keep warm. Strain off the liquid and

Braised goose

continued

skim thoroughly to remove the fat. Add the liquid to the brown sauce, then boil gently, to reduce, until it has a good flavour (5-6 minutes). Thicken if necessary with arrowroot slaked in a little cold water. Pour a little of this sauce round the goose and surround with the garnish of fried chipolata sausages and braised chestnuts. Serve remaining sauce in a sauce boat.

Braised chestnuts

Put 1 lb chestnuts in a pan, cover them with cold water and bring to the boil. Draw pan aside ; take out the nuts one at a time and strip off the outer and inner skin. When all the nuts are skinned, put them in a stew pan, cover with about $\frac{3}{4}$ pint jellied stock, season lightly, put the lid on the pan and simmer until the nuts are tender (about 20-30 minutes). Then take off the lid and increase the heat to reduce any remaining stock. The nuts should be nicely glazed.

Game birds

Large or small — and some are small enough to serve on a round
of toast — game birds are fit for the table of a king.
The infinite variety of flavours has been enjoyed for centuries,
and the birds preserved by the laws which protect them.
All Cordon Bleu cooks would do well to master the art of
preparing these special birds.

Preparation

Game is a term that covers wild birds and animals that are protected by law. Although pigeon and rabbit are not strictly game, for convenience they are sold on the same counter and are often prepared like game, which needs rather different handling from poultry.

All game needs hanging if the flesh is to be tender and well-flavoured. The length of hanging time allowed depends on personal taste and the weather.

Do not pluck or draw game before hanging. Birds are ready when the tail feathers are easy to pull and, if young ones, the best way to cook them is by roasting. Each kind of game has its classic accompanying dishes.

Preparation continued

Age of birds
To be sure that your bird is a young one, look first at the legs and feet ; these should be smooth and pliable. In the case of a cock bird, the spurs should be rounded and short with supple feet and toe-nails. The feathers on the breast and under the wing should be downy and soft, and the tips of the long wing feathers pointed ; rounded points indicate an older bird. The end tip of the breastbone should give slightly in a young bird.

Hanging
Game should be literally hung (ie. suspended from a hook), to allow the air to circulate freely around it. Hang it in a cool, dry place, such as an outside larder well protected from flies, or in a dry cellar. (A garage, toolshed or potting shed — if rat-free — would be good, but if not available, a well-ventilated larder would do, although it is better not to hang game near other food, which may pick up its strong flavour.) Feathered game is hung from the neck ; other game (hares and rabbits) by the hind legs.

To test if birds are ready for cooking, pull out a small tuft of feathers just above the tail ; this should come away easily. The bird may then be plucked, drawn and trussed ready for cooking. A green or bluish discolouration of flesh shows the bird has been hung too long.

Plucking
The poulterer (or butcher) plucks and draws game he sells, but you will have to do this for 'home-killed' game, although your local poulterer may do it for you for a small charge.

Plucking must be done carefully because the skin becomes soft and tender during hanging and it must not be torn.

For a small bird, spread it on newspaper to catch feathers.

For a large bird, place a board over a bin (or large container) and lay the bird on it. When you start plucking, the feathers will then fall straight into the bin. This is the easiest way to do it, especially with a downy bird (see photograph below).

To pluck a large game bird, such as a pheasant (shown below), lay it on a board over a bin so that the feathers fall into it. Hold bird firmly by legs, and pull out feathers in opposite direction to that in which they lie, using sharp jerks

Hold the bird firmly by the legs. Starting from the tail end and using a small, quick jerk, pull out the feathers, away from you, a few at a time, in the direction opposite to that in which they lie. Take particular care with feathers on the breast where the flesh is most tender.

To pluck the wing feathers, bend wing into a natural position. Grip all of the main feathers in one hand and then give them a sharp pull. This will extend the wing and nearly all the feathers should come out at one go. Then pull out any remaining feathers (you may need to use a pair of pliers).

When all the feathers are removed, singe off the remaining down. The best way to do this is to pour 1-2 tablespoons methylated spirit on to an enamel or fireproof plate and set alight. Then, holding the bird by the head and feet, turn it round in the flame. A gas flame

After plucking and singeing, lay bird on newspaper. Draw skin of neck up towards crop (at head end), slit around skin and insert two fingers ; loosen around crop and draw it out carefully. Next cut off neck close to body ; take remaining skin off neck. Cut off head, discard this and crop but reserve skinned neck for making the gravy

To draw contents of carcass, make a tiny slit just above vent to cut outer and inner skins. Insert two fingers, loosen around the contents, keeping your fingers on the sides. Reach up to crop end and, when you feel the heart, grasp it and gizzard (stomach) and draw out the contents in one go. (Skinned neck is shown on the left of bird)

Preparation continued

can be used in the same way, but it does not have such a wide area of flame. Hold and turn the bird as before, but don't swing it.

Drawing

All large game birds, such as pheasant, must be drawn before cooking ; some of the smaller birds are not drawn.

The best way to do this rather unpleasant job is shown in the photographs below. Drawing should be done in one operation, and you'll find it less messy if you wrap your hand in a damp cloth.

After drawing, wipe the bird inside and out with a damp cloth or absorbent paper before trussing it. Usually, the feet and legs are cut off just below the hock joints. Truss game birds as for poultry (see page 12) tucking the neck skin under the wing pinions.

After drawing out intestines, reserve gizzard (held below), heart and liver — these, and the neck, are the giblets. Carefully cut off gall bladder, which is attached to the liver, and then discard it ; do not break this bladder or else liver becomes bitter and must be thrown away. Discard remainder of intestines before cleaning the gizzard

To clean the gizzard, first carefully slit its outside curved edge until the tough inner skin or little sac is reached ; then fold back outer skin so that the sac can be detached and discarded (but reserve outer skin). If inner sac is broken (shown below), pull off outer skin and scrape out contents ; wash gizzard well and keep giblets in cold water

Roast game

brace of young birds
2 slices of fat bacon
2-3 oz butter, or bacon fat, or good
   beef dripping
salt and pepper
2 tablespoons plain flour (for
   dredging)

For gravy
stock (made from giblets, 1 carrot,
   1 onion, bouquet garni)
1 beef bouillon cube (optional)
1 teaspoon plain flour
watercress (to garnish)

Grouse, pheasant and wild duck are the most plentiful large game birds. This recipe is basic to cooking all these.

If the birds are bought from the poulterers, they will have a slice of larding fat tied over their breasts ; in this case, omit the fat bacon.

Method

To make stock : put the giblets in a pan, cover with water and add the vegetables, sliced, and bouquet garni to flavour. Simmer for 30-40 minutes. Since gravy served with all game should be well flavoured, a beef bouillon cube may be added to improve its flavour.

Set oven at 400°F or Mark 6.

Wipe insides of the birds with a damp cloth, but do not wash. Put a piece of butter (the size of a walnut) mixed with salt and pepper inside each bird and truss them with fine string or thread (see page 13 for diagrams).

Heat the rest of the butter or bacon fat in a roasting tin, put in the birds and baste well. Turn birds and baste while cooking so that their thighs and undersides are well coloured. Cooking times vary according to type.

Five minutes before dishing up, remove the fat bacon or larding fat, baste the breast well and dredge with flour. Baste again before returning to the oven for the final 5 minutes. This is known as 'frothing the breast' and gives the bird an attractive appearance. Now take birds out of oven, remove trussing strings and keep hot.

To make the gravy : pour off fat from roasting tin, leaving any sediment behind. Dust in a very little flour and blend it into juices in pan. Cook for 2-3 minutes, then tip on stock. Boil up, scrape sides of pan, reduce in quantity by boiling for 1-2 minutes, season and strain.

Serve birds garnished with watercress. Serve with the gravy, fried crumbs and bread sauce. Game chips should be served separately. See page 99 for accompaniments.

Gravy for game

1 lb chicken giblets (mixed necks
    and gizzards, and any game
    giblets available)
$\frac{1}{2}$ lb shin of beef
1 rounded tablespoon beef
    dripping
1 medium-size onion (sliced)
1 $\frac{1}{2}$ pints water
bouquet garni
6 peppercorns
1 small carrot (sliced)
1 teaspoon salt
1 clove

In recipes for roast game, it is always stressed that strong, clear gravy should accompany it, but you are rarely told how to prepare it. If roast pheasant or wild duck, for example, is served regularly, it's a good idea to make a quantity of good gravy and have it to hand. Ideally, the brown jelly or glaze found on the bottom of a cake of beef dripping is what you should use, but there is not usually enough of it.

The giblets, neck, gizzard and heart are used for making a little concentrated gravy to serve with a plainly roasted bird. The feet (like those from a chicken) should be blanched and scraped before adding to the giblets. The liver may be pounded and mixed with a little strong stock and wine to form the basis of a sauce for a salmis. When buying game, you should ask for the giblets.

The recipe for gravy given here makes 1 pint, and is one that can be deep frozen and used as needed.

Method
Wash and blanch the giblets, then dry them ; cut them and the beef into small pieces. Melt the dripping in a shallow pan, put in the onion, giblets and beef. Set pan on low heat and fry until all are lightly coloured.

Pour in about $\frac{1}{2}$ teacup of the water. Continue cooking gently, stirring occasionally, until the liquid has reduced to a brown glaze. Then add the remaining water and the rest of the ingredients. Bring gravy to the boil, then lower the heat and simmer, with pan lid slightly off the pan, for 1 hour. Then strain gravy and leave until cold ; skim off any fat.

Watchpoint Gentle simmering will keep the gravy clear ; boiling will make it cloudy. If the $\frac{1}{2}$ teacup of liquid first used can be good stock instead of water, the process of the liquid 'falling' to a glaze will be much quicker. The remaining liquid added may be water.

Orange gravy
(for 2 birds)

1 small onion (sliced)
$\frac{1}{2}$ oz butter
3-4 strips of rind and juice of
    1 Seville orange
$\frac{1}{4}$ pint good stock (see page 97)
1 port glass (2   fl oz) port, or
    red wine
pepper (ground from mill)
pinch of cayenne pepper
a little arrowroot (optional)

Method
Put the onion and butter into a small pan, allow to colour, then add orange rind and stock. Simmer for 10 minutes, then strain. Return to the pan and add the strained juice, port (or wine) and seasoning. Bring to the boil, thicken very slightly with the arrowroot, if necessary.

Accompaniments to roast game

Fried crumbs

8 tablespoons fresh white breadcrumbs
2 oz butter

Method
Heat the butter gently and skim
well. Increase the heat under
the pan, add the breadcrumbs
and stir until golden-brown.
Serve in a sauce boat, or small
gratin dish.

Bread sauce

4-6 tablespoons fresh white breadcrumbs
$\frac{1}{2}$ pint milk
1 small onion (stuck with 2-3 cloves)
$\frac{1}{2}$ bayleaf
salt and pepper
1 oz butter

Method
Bring the milk to the boil, add
onion and bayleaf ; cover pan ;
leave on side of stove for 15
minutes to infuse. Remove the
onion, add the breadcrumbs and
seasoning and return to heat ;
stir gently until boiling. Beat in
the butter, a small piece at a time
and serve hot.

Game chips

Choose large potatoes ($1\frac{1}{2}$ lb
will be sufficient for up to 6
people). Peel and trim off the
ends and cut in very thin slices.
Soak slices in a large bowl of
cold water for 1 hour, separating
slices to prevent their sticking
together. Drain well and leave
wrapped in a clean teacloth for
20 minutes, again separating
the slices so that they dry
thoroughly.

Fry the slices a few at a time
in a basket in deep fat or oil
heated to 350°F and remove
when bubbling subsides. When
all slices have been cooked in
this way, reheat the fat or oil to
375°F, put two or three batches
of slices together in the basket
and fry until they are golden-
brown.

As soon as there is no danger
of the fat bubbling over, turn
potato slices out of basket into
pan to finish cooking ; keep
them separated with a draining
spoon. Drain well on crumpled,
absorbent paper and then pile
on to a hot dish. Sprinkle with
salt and serve.

Watchpoint Never cover up
game chips or they will lose all
their crispness.

Cranberry sauce

1 lb cranberries
1 teacup of cold water
4 oz granulated sugar
about 1 tablespoon port (optional)

Method
Wash cranberries, put in saucepan, cover with cold water and
bring to the boil. Simmer,
bruising the cranberries with a
wooden spoon, until reduced
to a pulp.

Add sugar and port wine (if
using). Cook very gently until
all the sugar is dissolved.

Large game birds

Grouse
(Season : 12 August—
10 December)

Spit or oven roast young birds, at 400°F or Mark 6, for 35 minutes. Serve with browned crumbs, game chips and strong gravy, and either rowan or red-currant jelly. Bread sauce is not usually served, but you can offer cranberry sauce, in which case omit the jelly. One plump grouse should serve 2 people.

Black game
(Season : 20 August—
10 December)

A large bird, a species of grouse, about the size of a pheasant ; the cocks are black and the hens grey. Like grouse it is a native of hilly country and moors in Scotland and northern England. The flesh is like grouse in flavour but inclined to be a little dry. For that reason, lard it well before roasting and put a lump of butter inside the bird. Roast with butter and baste well during the cooking. Approximate roasting time is 40-50 minutes, though 35-40 minutes is usually sufficient for the smaller hen. Serve with the same accompaniments as for grouse.

Black game should be served slightly underdone, ie. with the flesh lightly pink. A good size bird is enough for 3-4 people.

Capercailzie, or wood grouse
(Season : 1 October—
31 January)

This large bird is also of the grouse family. It is now quite rare but was at one time found in the highlands and moors of Scotland. A 'caper' is a large bird (7-10 lb) with handsome plumage, the legs being feathered down to the toes, like grouse.

Hang for 7-10 days and roast as for black game.

Ptarmigan, or white grouse
(Season : 12 August—
10 December)

This bird, which is comparatively scarce, is similar to grouse and about the same size. Its plumage becomes white in winter. It has not quite the same flavour as grouse but is good in casserole dishes and others of the same type. Cook as for grouse.

Game mousse

$\frac{1}{2}$ lb cooked grouse
$\frac{3}{4}$ pint demi-glace sauce (see page 73)
1 rounded tablespoon tomato purée
2$\frac{1}{2}$ fl oz jellied stock (see page 97)
2$\frac{1}{2}$ fl oz Madeira wine
$\frac{1}{2}$ oz butter
salt and pepper
1 oz gelatine
2 tablespoons stock
$\frac{1}{4}$ pint aspic jelly
$\frac{1}{4}$ pint double cream (lightly whipped)

For decoration
2$\frac{1}{2}$ fl oz aspic jelly
1 tablespoon chopped truffle, or chopped, cooked mushroom

5 -inch diameter top (size No. 3) soufflé dish

Method

Prepare the soufflé dish with a band of greaseproof paper round the outside standing 3 inches above rim.

Add tomato purée to the demi-glace sauce and simmer for 5 minutes, then add 2$\frac{1}{2}$ fl oz jellied stock. Continue to simmer, skimming often, until well reduced. Then add the wine and beat in the butter.

Mince the grouse twice, pound it well and sieve or work in an electric blender with the sauce and seasonings.

Soak the gelatine in 2 table-spoons stock, then add the aspic jelly and dissolve it over gentle heat. Add to the grouse mixture and fold in the whipped cream. When the mixture is on the point of setting pour into the prepared dish and leave to set.

To decorate, add the chopped truffle (or mushroom) to the aspic jelly and pour over the top of the cold mousse, then chill again.

Marinated, jugged grouse

2 good, old grouse
scant $\frac{1}{2}$ pint stock (see page 97)
$\frac{3}{4}$ lb chuck steak
a little dripping
1 medium-size onion (finely chopped)
bouquet garni
1-1$\frac{1}{2}$ wineglasses port, or red wine
1 tablespoon redcurrant jelly (see page 154)
pinch of ground mace
forcemeat balls (see page 151)

Method

Split the grouse, trim away the backbones and add the bones to the measured stock. Put into a pan, cover and simmer for 20-30 minutes, then strain.

Set oven at 325°F or Mark 3. Cut the steak into $\frac{1}{2}$-inch pieces and brown quickly in a little hot dripping. Take out of the pan, add the grouse and the onion, lower the heat and allow just to colour. Then layer the steak and grouse together in a casse-role and season well. Tuck in the bouquet garni and pour over the prepared stock. Add 1 glass wine, redcurrant jelly and mace, cover tightly and cook in the pre-set oven. Pre-pare the forcemeat balls and set aside. After 1 hour's cooking, remove the casserole lid and place the forcemeat balls on top of the steak and grouse layers. Cover again and con-tinue to cook for a further hour, when the meat should be very tender. If wished, 10-15 minutes before the dish is ready, remove the lid and allow the forcemeat balls to brown. A small glass more of port can be poured into the casserole just before serving. Serve with braised red cabbage and creamed potatoes (see pages 153, 154).

Casserole of grouse

2 grouse
1 oz butter, or dripping
1 carrot
1 small turnip
2 onions
2-3 sticks of celery
$\frac{1}{2}$-$\frac{3}{4}$ pint stock (see page 97)
bouquet garni
1 wineglass red wine
salt and pepper
glazed onions (to garnish)

Method

Melt butter (or dripping) in a thick casserole, wipe grouse, brown slowly in butter. Remove grouse from casserole and keep hot.

Dice vegetables and sweat, ie. cook slowly in casserole until all fat is absorbed, then allow to colour slightly. Add stock, bring to boil, add bouquet garni, grouse and red wine, flamed. To flame wine, heat it gently in a small pan and set it alight. When flame burns out, alcohol will have evaporated. Season, cover pan tightly and cook slowly on top of stove for 40 minutes. Baste regularly with gravy.

Dish up grouse, remove bouquet garni and garnish with glazed onions (see page 152).

Grouse and hare pie

2 old grouse
1 lb beef skirt
$\frac{1}{2}$ hare (3-4 joints)
2 sheeps kidneys
2 oz flat mushrooms
forcemeat balls (see page 151)
1 small onion (finely chopped)
$\frac{1}{2}$ lb streaky bacon (blanched and diced)
$7\frac{1}{2}$ fl oz stock (made from the bones and trimmings — see method, page 97)
6 oz quantity of rich shortcrust pastry (see page 153)

8-9 inch diameter deep pie dish

Method

Split the grouse, and cut each half in two. Cut beef into strips, cut the hare joints in pieces or, if using the back, split through length. Skin and halve the kidneys lengthwise and chop the mushrooms. Prepare the forcemeat balls and set aside.

Set the oven at 400°F or Mark 6. Layer the meats, onion, bacon, kidneys and mushrooms into the pie dish, season well and arrange the forcemeat balls on the top, pour in the stock, cover with the pastry, trim round and decorate. Bake in pre-set hot oven for 25-30 minutes, then wrap in wet greaseproof paper, lower heat to 325-350°F or Mark 3-4 for a further $1\frac{1}{4}$ hours. Serve pie hot or cold.

Grouse and hare pie, covered with rich shortcrust pastry and decorated

Pheasant

(Season : 1 October—1 February)

This handsome bird was originally a foreigner to Great Britain but for some time past has been a native of our woodlands. It is the only game bird which is bred for shooting. Hen birds are as a rule more tender and succulent than the cocks. Pheasants, like most game, are sold by the brace, ie. a cock and a hen. Young birds may be spit or oven roasted for approximately 45-55 minutes. Cocks and slightly older birds should be pot roasted to keep them as moist as possible. The flavour of a pheasant goes well with a sub-acid such as apple, or sometimes even grapes or raisins. A pheasant lends itself to a variety of dishes, but if served plainly roast it must be well hung otherwise it can be dull and tasteless. Serve with sprouts or braised celery, fried or browned crumbs, bread sauce and game chips. A good size bird serves 4-5 people.

Pheasant Viroflay

2 hen pheasants
2 oz butter
1 dessert apple (sliced)
$\frac{1}{4}$ pint stock (see page 97)
1 wineglass white wine, or sherry
2 tablespoons double cream

For farce
1 shallot (finely chopped)
2 oz butter
$\frac{1}{2}$ lb green streaky bacon (boiled for about 45 minutes and minced)
1 teacup fresh white breadcrumbs
$\frac{1}{2}$ lb leaf spinach (blanched and chopped)
2 egg yolks
1 dessertspoon chopped thyme and sage (mixed)
salt and pepper

Trussing needle and fine string

Method

Cut the pheasant down the back, remove the carcass bones but leave in the leg and wing bones.

To prepare the farce : cook the finely chopped shallot in the butter until soft but not coloured and mix with all the other ingredients. Season well.

Set the oven at 400°F or Mark 6. Fill the birds with the farce, sew them up with fine string and truss neatly. Rub the birds with the butter and set in a roasting tin with the apple and stock. Cook for about 45 minutes in the pre-set oven, basting and turning from time to time. Take up the pheasants and deglaze the pan with the wine, boil up and strain. Carve the pheasants and arrange on a serving dish. Add the cream to the gravy and spoon it over the birds.

Stuffed pheasant alsacienne

1 plump pheasant
1½-2 oz butter (for roasting)
1 glass sherry
1 wineglass stock (see page 97)
bouquet garni
2-3 sticks of celery

For farce
1 medium-size onion (finely
   chopped)
good ½ oz butter
6 oz pork (minced)
2 tablespoons fresh white
   breadcrumbs
1 teaspoon chopped sage
salt and pepper
1 egg yolk

For sauce
2-3 cooking apples
½ oz butter
salt and pepper
caster sugar (to taste)
2-3 tablespoons cider
1 tablespoon arrowroot (slaked with
   2 tablespoons water)
2½ fl oz double cream

Trussing needle and fine string

This is served with an apple sauce flavoured with cider and with cream added. Also served separately are süsskraut and château potatoes (see page 153).

Method
Bone out the pheasant, leaving in the leg bones.

To prepare the farce : soften the onion in the butter. Add this to the pork with the breadcrumbs and sage. Season and bind with the egg yolk. Fill the pheasant with this stuffing, reshape, sew up and truss. Brown carefully in hot butter in a flameproof casserole, then flame with the sherry. Add stock, bouquet garni and sliced celery.

Cover tightly and simmer on low heat or in the oven at 350°F or Mark 4 for 45-50 minutes.

Meanwhile prepare the sauce. Slice the apples without peeling them and cook to a pulp with the butter. Rub through a strainer and return to the pan. Season and add sugar to taste, then pour on the cider. Simmer for 5 minutes.

Take up, carve and dish up the pheasant. Strain the gravy, add to the sauce with the cream and thicken it slightly with a little slaked arrowroot, spoon some over pheasant ; serve rest separately.

Süsskraut

1 small Dutch cabbage
1-2 oz butter
2 tablespoons wine vinegar
1 tablespoon caster sugar
salt and pepper
1 tablespoon chopped parsley

Method
Wash and shred cabbage finely. Well rub a thick pan with butter and pack in the cabbage, adding the vinegar, sugar and seasoning. Cover with buttered paper and the pan lid and cook slowly for 20-25 minutes until the cabbage is just tender. Fork in chopped parsley just before serving.

Pheasant vallée d'Auge

1 large pheasant, or 2 hen
  pheasants
$1\frac{1}{2}$ oz butter
2 medium-size apples (cooking or
  dessert apples)
1 medium-size onion (finely sliced)
2-3 sticks celery (sliced)
1 tablespoon plain flour
$1\frac{1}{4}$ glasses white wine
$\frac{1}{2}$-$\frac{3}{4}$ pint jellied stock (see page 97)
salt and pepper
1 small carton ($2\frac{1}{2}$ fl oz) double
  cream
chopped parsley

For garnish
1 head of celery
1 green pepper, or pimiento (cut
  into rings) — optional
2 Cox's apples
1 oz butter
caster sugar

This is one of the best of
pheasant dishes and is especially suitable for a party, in
which case use 2 hen pheasants.

Method
Brown the birds slowly and
carefully all over in the butter
in a flameproof casserole.
Meanwhile quarter, core and
slice the apples. When the
birds are browned take. them
out of the casserole and put in
the onion, celery, and apples ;
sauté gently for 5-6 minutes.
Stir in the flour, off the heat, and
add the wine and stock. Bring
to the boil, season and turn out
into a bowl. Put pheasants
back in casserole and pour over
sauce ; cover with greaseproof
paper or foil and the lid and
simmer on top of the stove or
cook in a moderate oven, pre-set
at 350°F or Mark 4, for 45-50
minutes.

Meanwhile prepare garnish.
Separate celery into sticks, cut
these into 2-$2\frac{1}{2}$ inch strips. Tie
in bundles, using a 4-5 inch
length of string for each one for
lifting out of saucepan. Cook
for about 12 minutes in boiling
salted water. Remove the string
and put a ring of pepper
around each bundle.

Wipe the second lot of apples,
cut crossways in $\frac{1}{4}$-$\frac{1}{2}$ inch thick
slices and stamp out the core
with an apple corer. Fry slices
quickly in butter and dust well
with caster sugar. Do this on
full heat and allow about $1\frac{1}{2}$-2
minutes on each side.

1 *Dusting the apple rings with sugar
for pheasant vallée d'Auge*
2 *Garnishing dish with celery
bundles, apple rings and potatoes*

When apples are browned, lift carefully on to a greased plate and keep hot.

Watchpoint If apple rings are overcooked, they become wrinkled and do not look very appetising when served.

When the birds are tender take them out of the casserole and strain the sauce, pushing as much of the vegetable and apple mixture through the strainer as possible. Turn into a saucepan, adjust the seasoning and boil up well. When a syrupy consistency, add the cream, whisking it well in. Leave to simmer while the birds are carved. Dish them up and spoon over enough of the sauce to coat nicely ; serve the rest separately. Garnish dish with celery bundles and apple rings. Dust with parsley, and serve château potatoes (see page 153).

Pheasant smetana

2 **pheasants (a brace, or 2 hen birds)**
good oz butter
2 **shallots (chopped)**
1 **glass white wine**
salt and pepper

For sauce
3 **shallots (finely chopped)**
1 **large wineglass dry white wine**
1 **dessertspoon plain flour**
$7\frac{1}{2}$ **fl oz lightly soured cream (fresh cream with a little lemon juice added may be substituted)**

Method

Heat the butter in a large pan and slowly brown the birds all over. Then add shallots and wine, season, cover and simmer gently on top of the stove for 35-40 minutes, turning the birds over from time to time.

When the birds are cooked, pour off the gravy from the pan and reserve it, leaving birds in pan, covered. To prepare the sauce, cook shallots in the wine in a saucepan until the wine has reduced by half, then pour off and set aside. Skim the butter from the reserved gravy, put it into the saucepan and stir in the flour. Strain in the gravy, add the reduced wine and the cream. Season well and boil until sauce is thick and creamy. Draw pan aside.

Take up pheasants, carve into joints and dish up. Reheat sauce and strain over the dish. Serve very hot with boiled rice (see page 28) and French beans.

Pheasant smetana is cooked in white wine with shallots. Its name comes from 'smetana', the Russian for soured cream which is used in the sauce

Galantine of pheasant

1 large plump pheasant
salt
pepper (ground from mill)
bouquet garni
root vegetables (sliced)
1 oz butter
$\frac{1}{2}$ glass sherry (for poaching)
1 wineglass jellied stock (see page 97), or canned consommé

For farce
6 oz minced veal, or pork
4 oz minced ham (cooked)
$\frac{1}{2}$ cup fresh white breadcrumbs
2 shallots, or 1 small onion (finely chopped)
$\frac{3}{4}$ oz butter
1 dessertspoon freshly chopped, or 1 teaspoon dried, sage
1 tablespoon chopped parsley
1-2 tablespoons sherry
pinch of ground mace, or nutmeg
1 small egg (beaten)

Trussing needle and fine string, or small skewer

This galantine should be partly made the day before it is needed.

Method
Slit the skin of the plucked pheasant down the back, then bone it out as for poultry (see page 13). Spread bird out on a board, cut side uppermost and season well.

To prepare farce : mix the minced meats and breadcrumbs together. Soften shallots (or onion) in $\frac{3}{4}$ oz butter without colouring, add to the meat mixture with the herbs and 1-2 tablespoons sherry. Add spice, seasoning and enough egg to moisten the farce but not to make it too wet. Spread farce on to the pheasant, roll it up neatly, and sew or fasten it with small skewers.

Break up the carcass bones, put them in a pan with water, bouquet garni and root vegetables to make some strong stock.

Heat a thick pan or flameproof casserole. Drop in about 1 oz butter, put in the pheasant and brown it all over slowly and carefully. Add $\frac{1}{2}$ glass sherry to pan and the same of pheasant stock. Season, cover tightly and cook gently for about 1 hour. Test if bird is cooked by running a thin skewer into the fleshy part of it. The time will vary according to the age of the bird ; an old bird will take up to about $1\frac{1}{2}$ hours.

When galantine is done, press it lightly between two plates. Deglaze the pan with the jellied stock or consommé, boil it up well, then strain and reserve.

Next day, remove any string or skewers from galantine. Glaze it with the reserved juices from the pan, added to a little of the pheasant stock, if necessary. The remaining stock can be reserved for a soup etc. Dish up galantine either whole or sliced, and serve with an appropriate salad, such as celery and apple, or orange and chicory, or celery and chestnuts with slices of fresh orange added.

Pot roast pheasant

1 pheasant
larding, or fat, bacon
1 oz butter
1 onion
1 carrot
bouquet garni
salt and pepper
$\frac{1}{2}$ cup stock (see page 97)
$\frac{1}{2}$ wineglass sherry (optional)

Pot roasting is a good way to cook some game such as pheasant, especially older birds which tend to be rather dry when roasted.

Method
Quarter the vegetables and cover the breast of the bird with larding, or fat, bacon. Heat the pot and drop in the butter. When foaming, put in the bird, surround with the vegetables and add bouquet garni. Season very lightly. Cover and cook for 5-6 minutes on moderate heat until vegetables begin to colour and steam starts to rise. Reduce heat and simmer gently for about 1$\frac{1}{2}$ hours.

To serve, take up pheasant and remove the larding bacon, dish up and keep hot. Remove bouquet garni, deglaze pot with $\frac{1}{2}$ cup of stock and then add, if you wish, the sherry. Season, strain and serve separately as gravy.

Alternatively, the pheasant may be carved and arranged in a serving dish. Spoon gravy over the bird and serve chosen vegetables separately. A vegetable that goes especially well with pheasant is braised cabbage with or without the apple. (See page 154).

Pheasant forestière

1 pheasant
1 oz butter
$\frac{1}{4}$ lb chipolata sausages (halved diagonally)
1 shallot (finely chopped)
6 oz green bacon rasher (cut into thick strips and blanched)
1 glass red wine
bouquet garni
4-6 oz button mushrooms (quartered)
1 wineglass stock (see page 97)
a little kneaded butter

Method
Brown the pheasant all over in the hot butter. Remove from the pan and add the sausages, shallot and bacon. When brown, remove sausages from pan and replace the pheasant, adding the wine and bouquet garni. Cover the pan tightly and simmer for 35-40 minutes, then add the mushrooms and sausages. Cover and cook for a further 7 minutes, then carve and dish up pheasant.

Add stock to the pan, first removing herbs, and thicken with kneaded butter. Boil up and spoon this sauce over pheasant. Garnish with glazed onions (see page 152).

Widgeon

**(Season : 1 September —
20 February — at its best
in November and December)**

This is the best of wild duck
and should be hung for about
3 days. After plucking and
drawing, cut off the neck close
to the body and draw the skin
over. Do not cut off the legs but
twist them at the knuckle and
lay the feet alongside the breast.
Then truss. Allow 1 bird for 2
people. Serve them lightly
roasted : spit or oven roast for
about 25 minutes — the meat
should be underdone. Froth the
breasts by removing fat bacon
or larding fat 5 minutes before
dishing up, basting breast well
and dredging with flour. Then
baste again before returning to
oven for final 5 minutes.

Serve with game chips, green
or orange salad (below) and a
strong clear gravy. Orange gravy
(see page 98) can accompany,
in which case serve green salad.

Orange salad

3 seedless oranges
French dressing (made with 1-2
   tablespoons white, or red, wine
   vinegar, 3-4 tablespoons olive oil)

Method

First pare off the rind of half an
orange, shred, blanch and
drain. Set aside. Then slice
away the peel and pith from the
oranges and cut into sections.
Arrange these in a small dish.
For dressing, mix vinegar with
seasoning, then whisk in the oil,
and spoon over salad. Scatter
over the blanched peel. Chill
slightly before serving.

Partridge

**(Season : 1 September
— 1 February)**

There are two varieties : the
English, or grey, partridge and
the French partridge, also
known as the Frenchman,
which is slightly larger than the
English one and has red legs.
The latter kind is Continental in
origin and is more common
than the English bird, especially
in the eastern counties of
England.

The English partridge is
especially prized for its flavour
when it is young, and cannot be
bettered when plainly roasted.
For perfection, spit or oven roast
it for 20-25 minutes and serve
with the traditional accompaniments of fried or browned
crumbs, strong, clear gravy,
game chips and bread sauce
(optional). It can also be stuffed
with mushrooms before roasting ; allow one plump bird per
person.

The French partridge is considered at its best when more
mature, being particularly suitable for stuffing or for any
made-up dish. Allow one
French partridge for two people,
if it is stuffed with a veal forcemeat and garnished.

Hang an English partridge for
3-4 days, a French one for 5-6
days ; older birds of both kinds
may need hanging for 1-2 days
longer. When trussing, it is
usual to tuck the feet inside the
body of the bird.

Most partridge and pheasant
recipes are interchangeable.

111

Partridge with black olives

3 plump partridges
1½-2 oz butter
4-6 oz green bacon rashers
3 shallots (finely chopped)
1 tablespoon plain flour
1 teaspoon tomato purée
½ pint well-flavoured, jellied stock (see page 97)
2 wineglasses red wine
salt and pepper
bouquet garni
3 oz black olives (stoned and halved)

Method

Set oven at 325-350°F or Mark 3-4. Brown the birds slowly and carefully all over in the butter. Meantime cut bacon into strips, blanch and drain. Add these to the pan with the shallots and continue to fry gently for 3-4 minutes, then remove the birds ; stir in the flour and add the tomato purée and the stock. Boil the wine in a small saucepan to reduce by about one-third and add to the casserole. Bring to the boil. Season, add the bouquet garni and replace the partridges.

Cover with a piece of paper or foil and then the lid. Cook in pre-set oven for 50-60 minutes, or until tender. Take up partridges, remove trussing strings, split in half and trim away some backbone. Arrange on a dish, boil the sauce rapidly for 2-3 minutes, or until syrupy, then add the black olives. Reboil sauce and spoon it over the dish at once.

Casserole of partridge

3 French partridges
½-¾ pint stock (see method)
1-1½ oz butter
¼ lb chipolata sausages
1 onion (sliced)
1 carrot (sliced)
1 rasher of bacon (blanched and diced)
1 dessertspoon plain flour
bouquet garni
4-6 croûtes of fried bread

For stuffing
1 shallot (finely chopped)
1 oz butter
3 oz fresh white breadcrumbs
1½ oz raisins (stoned)
1 oz chopped walnuts
1 teaspoon finely chopped parsley
1 small egg (beaten)
salt and pepper

Trussing needle and fine string, or poultry pins

Method

Bone out the partridges (as for chicken, see page 13) leaving the leg bones in, then spread out birds on your work surface. Clean the carcasses, break them up and use to make the stock, with vegetables and bouquet garni to flavour (see method page 153). Strain off required quantity and set aside.

Set oven at 325°F or Mark 3.

To prepare the stuffing : soften shallot in the butter, then mix with the remaining stuffing ingredients, binding mixture with the beaten egg and seasoning to taste. Spread stuffing on the partridges and sew up with fine string or secure with poultry pins.

Heat butter in a flameproof casserole, put in the sausages to brown slowly. Take them out and brown the partridges ; add the onion, carrot and bacon. Cook for 2-3 minutes, then dust with flour, add bouquet garni and reserved stock. Cover casserole tightly and braise slowly for 45-60 minutes in the pre-set oven.

When birds are tender, remove them from the casserole. Split them in half and serve each half on a croûte of fried bread. Cut sausages in half diagonally and add to the casserole. Spoon a little of the sauce and the sausages over each croûte and serve the rest separately, together with braised red cabbage (see page 154).

Casserole of partridge with red cabbage. The boned out birds are served on croûtes of fried bread

Partridge with cabbage (Perdrix au chou)

2 partridges
1 hard green cabbage (not Savoy),
   weighing 2 lb after washing and
   trimming
salt and pepper
6 oz green streaky bacon (in the
   piece)
1 oz bacon fat, or butter
piece of fresh pork rind (about
   6 inches by 4 inches)
2 medium-size carrots
4 oz pork sausages
1 large onion (stuck with a clove)
bouquet garni
1 pint stock (see page 97)
1 dessertspoon arrowroot (mixed
   with 1 tablespoon stock), or
   kneaded butter (made with 1 oz
   butter and 1 tablespoon flour
   — see page 157)

Method

Set oven at 325°F or Mark 3.

Cut the cabbage in four, blanch it in boiling salted water, drain and refresh, then squeeze it gently in a clean cloth. Cut each quarter into 2-3 pieces and season lightly between the leaves. Drop the bacon in cold water, bring to the boil, drain and refresh.

Heat the bacon fat in a heavy casserole, brown the birds on all sides and then remove them from the pan. Put the piece of pork rind, fat side down, at the bottom of the casserole and cover with a layer of cabbage, about one-third of the total quantity. Replace the part-ridges, arrange the whole carrots, bacon, sausages, onion and bouquet garni on top. Put the remaining cabbage in the pan, moisten it with the stock and season. Cover with a buttered paper and tightly fit-ting lid and put in pre-set mo-derate oven.

If the partridges are young birds, remove them from the casserole after 35 minutes. If old, they can remain in with the cabbage, which must be cooked for at least $1\frac{1}{2}$ hours.

Take out the sausages after 35 minutes and the bacon after 45 minutes. Keep these in-gredients covered to prevent them drying while the cabbage is completing its cooking time, but put them back again for 8-10 minutes before dishing up to make sure they are really hot.

To dish up, carve each partridge in four, cut the bacon in lardons and the sausages and carrots in rounds. Drain the cabbage in a colander over a saucepan, remove the onion and pork rind and then press the cabbage lightly to remove all the liquid. Place the cabbage in the serving dish, arrange the partridge on top and the bacon, sausage and carrot round the edge ; keep warm. Thicken the strained juices with the slaked arrowroot or kneaded butter, taste for seasoning. Spoon a little of this sauce round the cabbage and serve the rest in a sauce boat.

Ballotine of partridge

3 plump French partridges
1 shallot (finely chopped)
6 oz pork (minced)
3 rounded tablespoons fresh white breadcrumbs
1 tablespoon brandy
good pinch of dried thyme, or sage
salt and pepper
1 dessertspoon shredded pistachio nuts (blanched)
4 oz cooked tongue (sliced and shredded)
1 onion (sliced)
1 carrot (sliced)
2 sticks of celery (sliced)
about 1 pint aspic, laced with 2 tablespoons sherry (see page 150) — this will be enough to allow for chopped aspic as well as for brushing

For garnish
celery (shredded), or watercress

Trussing needle and fine string, or poultry pins

Method

Bone out the birds (see page 13), keeping in the leg joints. Add shallot to pork with breadcrumbs, brandy and herbs to make a forcemeat. Season cut surface of partridges, spread forcemeat on this and scatter the pistachio nuts and shredded tongue on the top.

Re-shape, sew up and truss (or pin) the birds, pressing the legs well into the sides. Wrap each bird in a piece of buttered foil (this will keep them moist) and simmer or braise with sliced onion, carrot and celery to flavour in a covered pan for 30-35 minutes.

Then take up partridges, lay them in a dish, cover with a board or another dish and weight it a little ; two 1 lb weights, separated, would be ideal. Leave birds until the next day, then remove weights, take birds out of the foil and remove trussing string (or pins) and carefully split them in half.

Arrange birds on a serving dish and brush well with aspic, which is on the point of setting. Garnish with shredded celery, or watercress, and a little chopped aspic.

Chopping aspic

When set, jelly should be turned on to a piece of wet greaseproof paper. Chop with a knife, but do not hold the point down as is usual when chopping parsley and other herbs. Avoid touching jelly with your hand as any form of grease will cloud it. Tilt the edge of the paper occasionally to move the jelly around, leave it coarsely chopped as it will sparkle better.

Jelly for chopping or cutting into blocks for garnishing may be set in shallow tins (sandwich tins, or ice trays with the sections removed) and chilled well in the refrigerator.

Partridges normande

2-3 partridges (according to size)
1½ oz clarified butter (see page 157)
2-3 shallots (finely chopped)
2 medium-size apples
(preferably Cox's, or Pippin)
2 tablespoons Calvados (apple brandy)
7½ fl oz jellied stock (see page 97)
bouquet garni
salt and pepper
about¼-½ oz kneaded butter (see page 157)
1 small carton (2½ fl oz) double cream
chopped parsley

Method

Heat a flameproof casserole, put in the butter, then the birds, breast-side downwards. Brown them slowly all over (this will take 7-10 minutes), then add the shallots and cook slowly, turning the birds every now and again, for a further 3 minutes. Quarter, core and slice the apples. Heat the Calvados, set it alight and pour flaming into the casserole. Add the stock, apples, the bouquet garni and seasoning. Bring to the boil and cook gently, either on top of the cooker or in the oven, pre-set at 325-350°F or Mark 3-4, for 45-50 minutes, or longer if the birds are not tender at the end of this time.

Watchpoint If the liquor in the pan evaporates too much, add a little extra stock during cooking.

Take up the partridges, remove the trussing strings and split each bird in half, trim away a little of the backbone with scissors and arrange on a serving dish. Turn the contents of casserole into a strainer, first removing the bouquet garni, and rub through. Return this liquid to the casserole, thicken very lightly with a little kneaded butter and, when boiling, add the cream. Boil hard for 1-2 minutes, then spoon sauce over the birds and sprinkle well with chopped parsley. Serve with château potatoes (see page 153).

Small game birds

Snipe
(Season : 12 August—31 January)

This is very much of a delicacy, and is seldom sold over the counter. Snipe is one of the smallest of game birds and is not drawn before cooking. Pluck, and strip off any skin from neck and head. Twist the head round and skewer the beak through the wing pinions. Flatten the legs close to the thighs and run a needle and string through to secure. Bard with a little fat bacon and grill quickly or put on a spit, skewering 3-4 together. Cook on full heat for 6-7 minutes. Snipe must 'fly through the kitchen' and the meat should be a rosy pink. Toast a small raft of bread for each snipe and place this on the bottom of the grill pan or on the tray under the spit to catch any drippings.

Serve each bird on a raft of toast ; allow 1-2 per person.

Woodcock
(Season : 1 October—31 January)

A much-prized bird and one which rarely, if ever, appears in the shops. It is larger than snipe, and is more the size of small grouse. Do not draw but truss as for snipe. Spit or oven roast ; if oven roasting, set the birds on a grid. Spread them well with butter and roast as for game for 15-20 minutes. For 2 birds, set rafts of buttered toast under them to catch the drippings. To serve, split in two and lay a half on each piece of toast. Serve with a strong gravy and game chips.

Pigeons and squabs

These are not game birds but are sold and often eaten in the same way.

Both wild and domesticated pigeons may be eaten. They are trussed in the same way as chickens except that the feet are left on — they are scalded and scraped and folded across the rear of the bird — and the wings are not drawn across the back. Squabs are very young pigeons, 4-6 weeks old. They are also specially bred for the table on squab farms and, being a pure breed, these are plumper and larger than the ordinary wood pigeon.

Watchpoint Cooking time in all pigeon recipes does depend on the age and size of the birds.

Teal
(Season : 1 September—20 February)

These birds are smaller than widgeon, so allow 1 per person. Hang for 3 days, then pluck and dress as for widgeon (see page 111). Roast, basting well with melted butter, allowing 15-25 minutes according to taste. Dish up on a raft of toast garnished with watercress and serve with orange gravy (see page 98), or combine and heat 1 oz butter, pinch of cayenne pepper and the strained juice of 2 lemons. When the teal are done, set on the toast, score the breast of each down to the bone at $\frac{1}{4}$-inch intervals. Pour over the sauce and serve at once.

Jugged pigeons

3 squabs, or 4 plump wood pigeons
2 onions (sliced)
½ pint brown ale, or cider
bouquet garni
½ pint good stock (see page 97)
kneaded butter (see page 157)
squeeze of lemon juice
chopped parsley (to garnish)

For stuffing
2 hard-boiled eggs
1 cup fresh white breadcrumbs
2 tablespoons shredded suet
pigeon livers
good pinch of ground mace
2 tablespoons chopped mixed herbs
  and parsley
1 small egg (beaten)
salt and pepper

Method

Set oven at 325-350°F or Mark 3-4. First prepare stuffing : push the yolks of the hard-boiled eggs through a strainer and add to the crumbs with the suet. Reserve the whites. Blanch and chop livers and add to yolk mixture with the mace, herbs and sufficient beaten egg to moisten ; add the seasoning.

Wipe the pigeons and stuff them with the mixture. Truss them and pack into a thick casserole with the onions. Pour over the ale (or cider), add the bouquet garni and half the stock. Bring to the boil, then put in pre-set slow to moderate oven for 1-2½ hours (1 hour for squabs, longer for wood pigeons) or until very tender.

Tip off the gravy into another pan and remove bouquet garni. Thicken the gravy with the kneaded butter and add rest of stock if necessary (there should be about ½-¾ pint of gravy in all). Add a squeeze of lemon and bring to the boil. If using squabs, take up and cut in half, first removing string. Leave the wood pigeons whole but re-move string. Pour over the gravy and serve in the casserole.

Shred the reserved egg white, scatter it over the top and sprinkle with parsley.

Pigeons in tomato sauce

4 pigeons
1 oz butter
1 large onion (sliced)
1 dessertspoon plain flour
4 oz mushrooms, or small can of mushrooms
$\frac{3}{4}$ pint tomato sauce (see method)

Method

Split pigeons in two, first cutting down to breastbone with a knife, then through bone and carcass with scissors. Trim away carcass bone. Slowly brown halves on skin side only in hot butter in a frying pan. Then take out halves and pack into a casserole. Set oven at 350°F or Mark 4.

Cook the sliced onion for 4-5 minutes in the pan, adding a little extra butter, if necessary. Take out onion and lay on top of pigeon halves in casserole.

If using fresh mushrooms, sauté briskly in pan of hot butter and set aside.

To prepare a quick tomato sauce : use a small can of Italian tomato sauce (not purée), make it up to $\frac{3}{4}$ pint with stock and thicken with kneaded butter or with a roux made with 1 dessertspoon flour and $\frac{3}{4}$ oz butter. Add to mushrooms. (If using canned mushrooms, add them now.)

Pour tomato sauce over pigeons, cover casserole tightly and cook in pre-set oven for 1-1$\frac{1}{2}$ hours or until pigeons are tender.

Pigeons casseroled in tomato sauce

Pigeons Saint-Germain

4 pigeons
2-oz slice of salt belly pork, or
  green streaky bacon
12 pickling-size onions (blanched)
1 tablespoon plain flour
$7\frac{1}{2}$ fl oz chicken stock (see page 156),
  or canned consommé
2 lb fresh green peas (shelled)
3 juniper berries, or pinch of
  ground allspice (Jamaica pepper)
sprig of thyme
salt and pepper
$7\frac{1}{2}$ fl oz apple juice

Method

Cut the pork or bacon into dice, put in a heavy casserole and place over gentle heat to draw out the fat. Add the pigeons and onions to the pan ; cook until brown on all sides, then remove from the pan. Blend in the flour, cook until russet-brown, pour in stock and stir until smooth.

Replace the pigeons and onions, add the shelled green peas, juniper berries, thyme and seasoning. Cover and simmer gently for about 40 minutes.

To serve : take up the pigeons, split in half and cut away the backbone and legs (these can be used to make a good game soup). Return the pigeon breasts to the casserole, pour on the apple juice and reheat. Taste for seasoning. The sauce should be the consistency of cream. Add extra thickening, if necessary ; either kneaded butter or slaked arrowroot.

Pigeons with raisins

4 pigeons
4-6 oz streaky bacon rashers
$1\frac{1}{2}$ oz butter
$\frac{1}{2}$-$\frac{3}{4}$ pint brown jellied stock (see page
  page 155)
16 button onions
caster sugar
2-3 oz stoned raisins (soaked in hot
  water for 30 minutes)

Method

Set oven at 325°F or Mark 3. Split pigeons in two and trim away the carcass bone with scissors.

Cut rashers into short strips, blanch (put in cold water, bring to the boil). Fry in the butter in a pan for 2-3 minutes, then take out and put in the pigeons. Brown slowly on skin side only. Take out halves and pack into a casserole with the bacon ; season and pour over the stock barely to cover. Bring to boil, cover tightly and cook for 1-1$\frac{1}{2}$ hours in the pre-set oven.

Meanwhile peel onions and brown in the pan, giving them a dusting of caster sugar. Add to casserole after first 30 minutes. Drain raisins and add to casserole 15 minutes before serving. At end of cooking time the gravy should be well reduced (brown and sticky). This is why jellied stock is essential, otherwise gravy will need thickening with kneaded butter or arrowroot.

Watchpoint Really good stock is essential to give a good rich sauce.

Pigeons en cocotte

4 pigeons
1 oz butter
4 oz green streaky bacon
12 small button onions
pinch of caster sugar
4 oz button mushrooms
$\frac{3}{4}$ oz plain flour
1 wineglass white wine
$7\frac{1}{2}$ fl oz chicken, or veal, stock (see 156)
salt and pepper

Method
Heat the butter in a deep pan, put in the pigeons and brown slowly and well on all sides. Set oven at 325°F or Mark 3.

Meanwhile remove rind from the bacon, cut into lardons and cover with cold water. Bring to the boil and simmer for 3 minutes ; drain and dry on absorbent paper. Blanch the onions ; drain and dry in the same way. Remove pigeons from the pan, add bacon and onions and cook carefully until nicely brown.

Watchpoint Remove the bacon with a draining spoon when brown and shake the pan to turn the onions without touching them, so that they remain whole. Add sugar to help them brown.

Remove onions from the pan with a draining spoon. Wash and trim mushrooms, cut in half and add to the pan ; cook briskly until brown, then remove from the pan. Stir in the flour, cook until golden-brown and add the wine and stock, blend until smooth and bring to the boil. Season, then strain sauce into a basin. Rinse and wipe out the pan and put back the pigeons, bacon, onions and mushrooms. Pour over the sauce and bring to the boil ; cover tightly and put in pre-set oven for 2 hours.

Pigeons en cocotte normande

4 pigeons
1 oz dripping, or butter
1 medium-size onion (sliced)
3 medium-size cooking apples
$\frac{3}{4}$ oz plain flour
$\frac{1}{2}$ pint stock (see page 155)
$\frac{1}{4}$ pint cider
salt and pepper
bouquet garni
4 rashers of streaky bacon
1 tablespoon chopped parsley (to garnish)

Method
Set oven at 350°F or Mark 4.

Brown the pigeons slowly in the dripping (or butter) in a flameproof casserole, then remove them from the pan, cut in half and trim away backbone.

Add the onion to the pan and allow it to colour. Wipe and core one of the apples, cut it in slices and put in the pan with the onion ; increase the heat and continue cooking until brown. Dust in the flour, cook for a further 2 minutes and then pour on the stock and cider. Bring to the boil, season, add bouquet garni and the pigeons. Cover the casserole tightly and cook in pre-set oven for $1\frac{1}{2}$ hours.

Take up the pigeons and arrange them in an entrée dish. Strain the sauce, reduce it over quick heat if too thin, and then spoon it over the pigeons. Cut the remaining apples in thick slices (about $\frac{1}{2}$ inch), and stamp out the cores with a small pastry cutter. Fry the bacon rashers until brown and crisp and place them on top of the pigeon. Fry the apple rings in the bacon fat very quickly until brown. Arrange the apple rings round the pigeons and dust with the parsley.

Stuffed pigeons St. Cyr

4 pigeons
$1\frac{1}{2}$ oz butter
1 wineglass white wine
$\frac{1}{4}$ pint strong veal stock (see page 155)
salt and pepper

For stuffing
2 oz mushrooms
2 oz butter
$\frac{1}{2}$ lemon
6 oz raw minced veal, or lean pork
2 oz tongue (chopped)

For garnish
2 lb green peas
1 lettuce heart (washed and quartered)
2 oz butter
salt and pepper
2 teaspoons caster sugar
4 tablespoons water
$\frac{1}{2}$ lb small new carrots
12 small button onions
4 slices of cooked tongue

Trussing needle and fine string

1 *Cutting rib cage away from pigeon.*
2 *Arranging vegetable garnish*
3 *Finished dish of stuffed pigeons St. Cyr with the birds placed on slices of tongue and vegetable garnish arranged in the centre*

Method

Set oven at 350°F or Mark 4. Cut the pigeons down the back, remove back and carcass bone.

To prepare the stuffing : trim and wash the mushrooms, chop finely and put in a pan with 2 oz butter and a good squeeze of lemon ; cover and cook for 5 minutes. Then allow to cool. Mix the minced veal (or pork), tongue and cooked mushrooms together and season well. Fill the pigeons, sew and truss neatly.

Melt the $1\frac{1}{2}$ oz butter in a deep cocotte and brown the birds slowly on all sides, season lightly, cover the pan tightly and put in pre-set moderate oven for about $1\frac{1}{4}$ hours.

Meanwhile prepare the garnish. Shell the peas and place in a casserole with the quartered lettuce heart, 1 oz of the butter, salt and pepper, 1 teaspoon sugar and 4 table-spoons water. Cover and cook gently for 15 minutes. Cut and trim the carrots into small 'barrels', cover with water, add 1 oz butter, 1 teaspoon suar and a little salt. Cook until all the water has evaporated, then shake the pan gently, turning the carrots until they begin to

colour in the butter and sugar glaze.

Cover the onions with cold water and boil for 5 minutes, drain, add to the pan with the peas and lettuce and continue cooking for 10 minutes. Cut the cooked tongue slices in half, place them on a plate and heat over the pan of peas.

To serve : take up the pigeons, remove the string, cut in half and press the stuffing in well ; arrange in a circle on a round dish with a slice of tongue between each pigeon half. Place the peas and onions in the centre and pile the carrots on top ; keep warm. Deglaze the cocotte with the white wine, stir briskly over the heat for 1 minute then add the veal stock ; season and spoon sauce over the pigeons.

Squabs St. Hubert

3 squabs
1½-2 oz butter
2 wineglasses red wine
1 tablespoon redcurrant jelly (see page 154)
1 oz almonds, or cashew nuts

For pilaf
8 oz long grain rice
1 medium-size onion
1-1½ oz butter
1-1¼ pints veal, or game, stock (see page 155)
salt and pepper
2-3 dried apple rings
2 oz dried apricots (soaked overnight with apple rings)
1-1½ oz currants (soaked in hot water for 30 minutes)

Method

Set oven at 350-375°F or Mark 4-5. Spread the pigeons with about 1½ oz of butter, put them in a small roasting tin and pour in 1 glass of wine. Roast them in pre-set oven for about 25-35 minutes, increasing the heat to 400°F or Mark 6 during the last 5 minutes of cooking; let them brown thoroughly.

To prepare the pilaf: chop the onion finely and sauté gently in 1 oz of butter in a flameproof casserole until just coloured, then add the rice and stir well. Add about 1 pint of the stock, season and bring to the boil. Cover and put casserole in the oven, under the pigeons, for about 12 minutes or until barely cooked.

Meanwhile prepare the dried fruit; cook the apricots and apples for about 10-15 minutes in the water in which they have

Layering dried apricots and apple rings on cooked rice for pilaf

Arranging the halved squabs around the pilaf on serving dish

been soaked, then drain them and cut into pieces. Drain the currants. Stir the fruit into the rice carefully with a fork. If the rice is dry, moisten it with a little of the stock. Season well and dot with the remainder of the butter. Cover with foil and a lid and put into the oven on the lower shelf. Leave for 15-20 minutes, forking the rice once or twice.

When the rice is dry, remove it from the oven. Take up the pigeons, split them and trim away the backbone. Make a gravy in the pan with the remaining glass of wine and some of the stock, finish with the redcurrant jelly and boil up well. Strain. Have ready the nuts fried in a little butter until brown. The rice can be served separately, otherwise dish up by turning on to the serving dish and arranging the pigeons around. Spoon a little of the gravy over the pigeons and serve the rest in a sauce boat. Scatter the nuts over the dish and serve very hot.

Squabs St. Hubert, served on a pilaf with fried almonds

Beefsteak, pigeon and mushroom pie

2 pigeons
1 oz butter
1½ lb shin of beef (cut into 1-inch squares)
2 pints chicken stock (see page 156)
salt and pepper
½ pint aspic jelly (commercially prepared)
¼ lb flat mushrooms
8 oz quantity of flaky, or puff, pastry (see page 152)
1 egg (beaten)
pinch of salt

9-inch long pie dish

Method

Melt the butter in a large stewpan, add the pigeons and brown slowly. Remove from the pan, split in half and return to the pan with the squares of beef and the stock. Season with salt and pepper, cover and cook slowly on top of the stove for 2-2½ hours.

Then cut the breast meat from the pigeons and discard the carcass ; add the aspic to the pan, turn out into a bowl and leave to get cold. Wash and trim the mushrooms, cut in quarters and put in a pie dish with the cooked meats and liquid. Place a pie funnel in the middle of the dish.

Set oven at 425°F or Mark 7.

Roll out the pastry to an oblong just under ¼-inch thick and about 3 inches wider and 4 inches longer than your pie dish. Cut off extra pastry ; roll these trimmings to ⅛-inch thick. From this thinner pastry, cut strips to fit on the rim of the pie dish, and make leaves and a thistle, or rose, for decoration. Dampen the rim of the pie dish and cover with a strip of pastry, pressing it firmly in position, then brush the pastry with cold water. Lift the thicker piece of pastry on your rolling pin and lay it carefully over the top of the pie, taking care not to stretch it. Trim it and press the two layers of pastry on the rim very firmly together ; seal and flute the edges.

Add a large pinch of salt to the beaten egg and beat lightly with a fork until the salt dissolves and the egg darkens in colour, this will give the pastry a rich brown and shiny glaze. Brush the top of the pie with the prepared egg wash, decorate suitably with pastry leaves, make a hole in the pastry in the centre of the leaves (above pie funnel) to allow for the escape of steam during cooking time. Brush the decoration with egg wash. Cook the rose or thistle on a baking sheet and put on pie when cooked.

Bake in pre-set oven for about 20-25 minutes, until pastry is cooked. While the pie is still warm add a little more liquid aspic through hole in centre, if necessary. Serve cold.

Putting cooked pigeon breasts, beef and mushrooms into pie dish

Jellied game

3 pigeons
1 rabbit
'wings' and legs of a hare (about
   1 lb), or equivalent weight of
   venison, or lean pork
1 pheasant, or any game bird
1 large onion (peeled)
1 carrot
large bouquet garni
strip of lemon rind
salt and pepper
$\frac{1}{2}$ lb cooked ham (sliced)

For forcemeat balls
$\frac{3}{4}$ lb pork sausage meat
1 tablespoon chopped parsley
2 tablespoons fresh white breadcrumbs
1 egg white (lightly stirred)
stock (for poaching)

For jelly
stock (from the game — see method)
1 glass golden sherry, or port, per
   quart of stock (optional)
scant 1$\frac{1}{2}$ oz gelatine

This quantity serves 8 people.

Method
Wipe all the game and put into
a large pan. Add peeled onion
and carrot whole, bouquet
garni and lemon rind. Season
and just cover with cold water.
Cover pan and simmer for 1$\frac{1}{2}$-2
hours until game is tender.

Meanwhile prepare force-
meat balls ; mix meat, parsley,
crumbs and season ; bind with
egg white. Shape into balls, lay
in a wide shallow pan (only one
layer). Just cover balls with
stock or water, put lid on pan,
poach gently for 12-15 minutes.
Remove from heat, leave in the
liquid to cool, then lift out.

Take game from pan, pull into
small slices with two forks,
discarding any skin or bones.
Strain the stock and return to
pan. Add the sherry or port and
extra seasoning, if necessary ;
reduce by boiling gently until
strong and well-flavoured.
Dissolve gelatine in 1 quart of
this stock. Allow to cool.

Layer game, shredded ham
and forcemeat balls in dishes.
Gently pour in enough of cool
jellied stock just to cover. Leave
until next day to set, or keep up to
2-3 days in refrigerator.

Watchpoint. Make sure that
game simmers but doesn't boil,
and when stock reduces that it
doesn't boil hard and cloud
jelly. Keep well skimmed.

Venison

As deer become scarcer, so it becomes rarer to see venison on the table.

Most of the venison now sold in Britain comes from Scottish moors. Not an easy meat to cook, because it tends to be rather dry, venison will well repay careful preparation. As you will see, this is not the dish for the last-minute cook.

Venison (Season: late June to January)

There are three different varieties of deer — fallow, roe and red — and venison can be the meat of any one.

Fallow are the domestic, or park, deer ; the roe or roebuck is found in woodlands ; the red deer in the high hills and mountains of Scotland. From time to time deer have to be 'culled' or thinned to keep the herd sound and healthy, so the meat can be bought at various times of the year from a butcher or poulterer.

Buck venison (considered the best) is in season only from late June until late September, but doe meat remains in season throughout November and December. The meat of both roe and fallow deer is good and, as the animals are smaller than the red, makes nice-size joints. The red deer has especially lean meat with a gamey flavour and must be well hung. This is normally done before it reaches the consumer, the usual time of hanging being 8-10 days, according to taste and, of course, the weather. Fallow and roe deer do not need so long.

As there is little natural fat on venison and the meat is inclined to be dry, additional moisture and flavour are given in the form of a marinade, a mixture of wine, oil, herbs, and spices. The meat can be marinated from 24 hours up to 3 days or even longer, again depending on personal taste. The best parts are saddle and haunch. Other pieces, such as cuts from the shoulder, are best jugged, or stewed.

Braised venison

3 lb venison (from the haunch)
marinade for venison (see venison
    sauté St. Hubert, page 134)
pared rinds of 1 orange and
    1 lemon

To braise
dripping (for browning)
2 onions (diced)
2 carrots (diced)
2 sticks of celery (diced)
bouquet garni
½ pint good stock (see page 155)
salt and pepper
1 tablespoon redcurrant jelly (see
    page 154)
kneaded butter (to thicken)

Method

Wipe the meat, put into a deep dish and pour over the cold marinade ; add rinds. Put prepared vegetables on top and cover with a lid. Leave 2-3 days in a cool place, turning venison occasionally.

When ready to cook, take meat out of marinade, wipe it with a cloth, then brown all over in a pan in the hot dripping. Remove, and put in the mirepoix of diced vegetables. Cover and cook gently for 7 minutes, then add venison, bouquet garni, strained marinade and stock.

Season, bring to boil, cover meat with a piece of greaseproof paper or foil, then the lid, and braise gently for 2-3 hours or until very tender in oven at 325°F or Mark 3.

Strain off the gravy, skim well to remove fat, add the redcurrant jelly and thicken with the kneaded butter. Reduce by boiling, if necessary, until sauce is the consistency of thin cream. Taste for seasoning. Slice the cooked venison, put in serving dish and spoon over the sauce.

131

Fillets of venison poivrade

1½ lb boned loin of venison (weighed without bone), or slices from the top of the haunch
a little oil
2½ fl oz red wine, or port
pepper (ground from mill)
2 tablespoons of peanuts, or cashew nuts
2 oz stoned raisins (soaked in hot water for 30 minutes)
6 croûtes of stale bread (cut into heart shapes and fried in a little hot oil)

For sauce poivrade
1 small onion (diced)
1 small carrot (diced)
1 small stick of celery (diced)
2-3 tablespoons oil, or dripping
1 tablespoon plain flour
1 oz mushroom stalks and / or peelings
1 rounded teaspoon tomato purée
bouquet garni
1 pint jellied stock (see page 155)
1 wineglass red wine
2 tablespoons red wine vinegar

Method

Slice the venison into strips $\frac{3}{4}$ inch thick. Lay them on a plate. Sprinkle with the oil and wine (or port) and grind over plenty of pepper. Cover and leave for about 1 hour.

Meanwhile prepare the sauce. Add the vegetables to the hot oil (or dripping) and cook gently until barely coloured. Add the flour and continue to cook slowly to a good brown. Then add the chopped mushroom stalks and / or peelings, tomato purée and bouquet garni, two-thirds of the stock, and the wine. Bring to the boil and simmer, with the pan partly covered, for 20-25 minutes. Then add half the remaining stock, reboil and remove any scum as it rises. Then add the rest of the stock and repeat this process. Strain the sauce, return to a clean pan, add the vinegar and continue to boil gently for a further 6-7 minutes. Draw pan aside.

Heat the nuts and stoned raisins in a little butter. Take out and set aside.

To cook the venison, reheat the pan, wipe the pieces of meat and sauté them briskly in a little hot oil or dripping, allowing about 4 minutes on each side. Then dish them up on a hot dish 'en couronne' with a croûte between each steak.

Note : start with a croûte on the dish, then a steak, then another croûte and so on, ending with a croûte.

Reboil the sauce and add the raisins and the nuts. Put several spoonfuls of the sauce into the centre of the dish and serve the rest separately.

Slicing venison before marinating in red wine, oil and pepper

Fillets of venison poivrade, served with a sauce, raisins and nuts

Venison sauté St. Hubert

1½-2 lb loin of venison
pork fat, or larding bacon (cut into
   lardons)
1 tablespoon oil
½ oz butter
1 small can Cape gooseberries

For marinade
2 wineglasses red wine
1 onion (sliced)
1 carrot (sliced)
1 large bouquet garni
6-8 peppercorns
2 tablespoons olive oil
1 dessertspoon red wine vinegar

For sauce
1 tablespoon finely sliced onion
1 tablespoon finely sliced carrot
small piece of celery
2 tablespoons oil
1 tablespoon plain flour
¾ pint jellied stock (see page 155)

Method
Bone the venison and cut into small steaks about ½-¾ inch thick. Combine all the ingredients for the marinade, bring to the boil, then leave till cold ; pour over the venison in a large dish and leave overnight.

To prepare the sauce : cook the vegetables in the hot oil until soft. Add the flour and cook slowly to a good russet-brown. Pour on ½ pint of the stock and simmer for 30 minutes. Add half the remaining cold stock, skim well, then simmer again for 5 minutes. Repeat this process using the rest of the stock, then strain.

Take up the venison steaks, pat dry and thread with the lardons of pork fat, using a larding needle. Strain the marinade, reduce by half in a pan on quick heat and add to the sauce.

Heat the oil in a sauté pan, add the butter and, when foaming, put in the venison and sauté for about 3½ minutes on each side, add a spoonful or so of the sauce and 2 tablespoons of gooseberries and heat carefully. Dish up venison and spoon over a little extra sauce. Serve with cabbage stuffed with chestnuts and creamed potatoes (see page 153).

Cabbage stuffed with chestnuts

1 firm green cabbage
1 lb chestnuts
1 onion (sliced)
1 oz butter
1¼ pint jellied stock (see page 155)
about ¼ pint brown sauce
   (preferably from venison)

Method
Trim the cabbage, removing any damaged outside leaves, and plunge in boiling salted water for 5 minutes, tip into a colander and refresh with cold water. Remove the inner and outer shell of the chestnuts (see braised chestnuts, page 90) and put the nuts in a pan with the onion, butter and 1 pint of jellied stock ; cover and cook gently until the chestnuts are tender and the stock has evaporated.

Curl back the outer leaves of the cabbage, scoop out the centre and fill with the chestnuts. Reshape the cabbage and fit it into a buttered casserole, pour over ¼ pint of the stock, cover and cook in oven, pre-set at 350°F or Mark 4, for 45-50 minutes. Spoon over the brown sauce and return to the oven for 5-10 minutes.

Venison ardennaise

$2\frac{1}{2}$-3 lb haunch, or saddle, of venison
pork fat, or larding bacon (cut into
  lardons)
1 tablespoon dripping
1 lb large onions (finely sliced)
$\frac{1}{2}$ pint brown ale
$\frac{1}{2}$ pint stock (see page 155)
1 clove of garlic (crushed with salt)
1 teaspoon red wine vinegar
1 teaspoon caster sugar
bouquet garni
black pepper (ground from mill)
1 dessertspoon French mustard
1 tablespoon double cream
1 tablespoon plain flour
1 can (8 oz) chestnut purée
salt
$\frac{1}{2}$ oz butter

For croquettes of celeriac
1 head of celeriac
seasoned flour
beaten egg
dried white breadcrumbs
butter (for frying)

Method

Set oven at 350°F or Mark 4. Lard the venison on one side only. Heat the dripping in a heavy flameproof casserole and brown the onions slowly. When they are really well coloured set the venison on the top, pour over the ale and stock and add the garlic, vinegar, sugar and herbs. Season well with black pepper, cover the pan and cook in pre-set oven for 1-1$\frac{1}{4}$ hours. Remove the lid of the pan, baste the meat, continue cooking for about 15 minutes uncovered, then remove meat from the pan and set on a baking sheet.

Mix the mustard and cream together, spread over the venison and return to the oven until the lardons are crisp. Meanwhile skim all the fat from the gravy in the pan and mix it with 1 tablespoon flour. Strain the gravy and reserve the onions. Stir the flour and fat into the gravy and reboil. Set aside.

Heat the chesnut purée, and add the onions, season well and add a nut of butter. Lay this down the centre of a serving dish, slice the venison and arrange on the top. Spoon over the gravy and garnish with croquettes of celeriac.

To prepare the croquettes : peel the celeriac and cut into wedge-shape pieces, simmer in salted water until barely tender. Drain well, leave till cool and then roll in seasoned flour, brush with beaten egg, then coat well with the breadcrumbs. Fry in butter until golden-brown.

Venison grenadins (steaks)

1½-2 lb loin of venison
pork fat, or larding bacon (optional)
butter
1 dessertspoon juniper berries

For marinade
2 wineglasses red wine
1 onion (sliced)
1 carrot (sliced)
1 large bouquet garni
6-8 peppercorns
2 tablespoons olive oil
1 dessertspoon wine vinegar

For sauce
1 tablespoon finely diced onion
1 tablespoon finely diced carrot
½ stick celery
2 tablespoons oil
1 tablespoon plain flour
¾ pint brown bone stock (see
    page 155)
1 tablespoon redcurrant jelly (see
    page 154)

Method
Bone the venison, tie up neatly, then cut across into 'grenadins', ie. steaks similar to a tournedos and as thick (1-1½ inches). These may be larded with pork fat, if wished. Combine all ingredients for the marinade and bring to the boil, then leave till cold. Spoon this over the grenadins in a dish and leave for several hours or overnight.

To prepare the sauce : barely colour the vegetables in the hot oil, add flour and cook slowly to a russet-brown. Add the stock and cook gently for 30-40 minutes. Skim well and strain, then return to the pan.

Take up the grenadins and dry them carefully. Strain marinade into the sauce, continue to simmer, skimming from time to time. Add the redcurrant jelly and simmer until syrupy.

Meanwhile sauté the grenadins in butter for about 3½ minutes on each side, adding the juniper berries once the grenadins have been turned. Dish up the grenadins and spoon over a little of the sauce. Serve the rest separately. Accompany the grenadins with chestnut croquettes.

Chestnut croquettes

1 can (8 oz) chestnut purée
2 shallots (chopped)
½ oz butter
salt and pepper
1 small egg (beaten)
seasoned flour
dried white breadcrumbs and
    beaten egg (for frying)

Method
Soften the shallots in the butter. Mix them with the chestnut purée. Season well. Bind with the egg. Shape into marbles and coat with flour, then egg and crumbs. Fry in deep fat until golden-brown.

Hare
and rabbit

Let someone else catch your hare or rabbit, but a good one, once caught, is well worth the attention of a Cordon Bleu cook. Since disease almost wiped out British rabbits, these long-legged creatures have been forgotten as table delicacies ; but the species is now fully recovered and the flavour of fresh, wild rabbit and hare is once again becoming known. The best dishes are the braises and casseroles that moisten the meat and retain every drop of the delicious juices.

Hare (Season : August — February)

There are two types of hare, ie. the English or brown hare and the Scots or blue hare. The former is considered to have the better flavour. A young hare is called a leveret.

A hare is at its best when young (up to its second year). The male is called a buck and the female a doe. The French call a young leveret up to three months a financier, up to six months a trois-quarts, and at a year a capucine or lièvre pit.

Preparation of hare

The best parts of a hare are the back and the legs. These may be used sautéd or roasted.

The wings (forelegs) of the hare are usually divided into two or three pieces, are braised or jugged with the rib-cage, and sometimes the shank part of the leg. If the hare is not very large the whole may be jugged.

The hare should be jointed, the legs cut in two and the back into 3-4 pieces. With scissors trim away the rib cage and the flaps of skin that are attached to the pieces of back. Do not wash but wipe well. The joints can then be marinated which greatly improves the flavour and texture of the meat. If buying the whole hare rather than a few joints, ask for the blood as well. This is used to thicken the sauce.

If the hare is freshly killed it should be hung for 8-12 days according to the weather, head downwards, so that the blood can collect in the rib cage, or thorax. Take care when skinning or jointing the hare not to break the membrane in the rib cage until you have a container ready to hold the blood. If marinating the hare, keep the blood in the refrigerator ; 1-2 drops of vinegar added to it will prevent it from clotting.

Unlike rabbit, hare is not drawn or paunched until after hanging.

Hare in beer

1 hare (jointed)
½ pint brown ale
1 clove of garlic (crushed with salt)
1 bayleaf
4 large onions (finely sliced)
¼ teaspoon grated nutmeg
1 tablespoon plain flour
1 teaspoon paprika pepper
1 tablespoon beef dripping
½ pint stock (see page 155)
1 teaspoon red wine vinegar
1 carrot (grated)
6 potatoes
little extra dripping, or butter

Method

Wipe the hare joints, put them in a large mixing bowl and cover with the beer, garlic, bayleaf, sliced onions and nutmeg. Mix together, cover and leave to marinate in the refrigerator for 24 hours.

Set oven at 350°F or Mark 4. Remove the pieces of hare from the marinade and wipe dry on absorbent paper; roll them in the flour mixed with the paprika. Heat the dripping in a flameproof casserole, put in the joints of hare and brown slowly over moderate heat. Blend in the stock and vinegar and add the marinade, including the onions and herbs. Add the grated carrot and bring to the boil. Cover the pan and put in pre-set oven for about 1¼ hours.

Boil the potatoes, cut in ¼-inch slices and arrange them on the top of the hare. Baste them with a little of the stock in the pan, dot with a few pieces of dripping or butter and return to the oven and continue cooking uncovered for a further 30-40 minutes or until the potatoes are quite soft.

Terrine of hare

For pastry
14 oz plain flour
2 oz lard
5 oz butter
2 small eggs (beaten)
1 teaspoon salt

For filling
1 young hare
3 tablespoons sherry, or brandy
salt
pepper (ground from mill)
pinch of ground mace
12 oz minced pork
3 oz bacon fat, or fat bacon (minced)
4 oz sausage meat
liver (chopped) and blood of hare
1 teaspoon dried marjoram, or oregano
1 tablespoon freshly chopped parsley
about ¼ pint jellied bone stock (see page 155)

8-inch spring-form mould

Method

First prepare the pastry: sift the flour on to a board or table, make a well in the centre and in this place the fats, beaten egg and salt, keeping back enough egg to glaze. Using the fingers of one hand, work up ingredients together until a smooth paste is formed. If necessary, add 1-2 tablespoons of cold water but be careful not to get the paste too wet. Set aside in the refrigerator for an hour.

Set oven at 400°F or Mark 6. To prepare the filling: cut the meat from the joints of the hare and slice it into neat shreds. Any wings or rib cage of hare left from another recipe may also be used. Put the meat in a dish and pour over the sherry (or brandy). Season well with salt, freshly ground pepper and mace. Mix the pork and bacon and the sausage meat with the liver, blood and herbs to make farce.

Roll out the pastry and line two-thirds of it into the mould. Fill it with a layer of the farce, then half the hare, then more farce ; finish with the remaining hare and top with the rest of the farce. Smooth over and cover with pastry, making a small hole in the top ; decorate with pastry trimmings and brush lightly with beaten egg. Bake for about 45 minutes in pre-set hot oven until pastry is well browned, then wrap it in a double sheet of dampened greaseproof paper. Lower the heat to 325°F or Mark 3 and continue to cook for about a further 45-50 minutes. Take terrine out of oven and pour in jellied stock. Serve cold.

Terrine of hare, cut open to show layers of farce and hare in jellied stock

Jugged hare

legs and wings of hare, or 1 hare
jointed (with the blood)
marinade (optional — see below)
1 tablespoon dripping
2 onions (diced)
2 carrots (diced)
1 stick of celery (sliced)
bouquet garni
salt and pepper
1½ pints stock (see page 155), or
water
1 tablespoon redcurrant jelly,
preferably home-made (see page
154)
1 small glass port wine
1 teaspoon arrowroot (to thicken),
or kneaded butter (see page 157)

For forcemeat balls
1 oz butter
1 shallot, or small onion (finely
chopped)
1 teacup fresh white breadcrumbs
1 dessertspoon dried herbs
1 dessertspoon chopped parsley
salt and pepper
beaten egg, or milk (to bind)

For frying
seasoned flour
1 egg (beaten)
dried white breadcrumbs
deep fat bath

For jugged hare it is not essential to marinate the meat before
braising, but this soaking will
improve the finished dish. Prepare marinade as for venison
marinade on page 134, using
2 tablespoons of red wine vinegar, and adding 2 strips of pared
lemon rind and 6 crushed
juniper or allspice berries.

Method

Marinate hare overnight. Then
drain and strain marinade.
Braise the hare. Heat the
dripping in a pan, brown the
meat, then remove from pan
and add the onion, carrot and
celery. Cook gently for 5-7
minutes, then put back the meat
with bouquet garni and seasoning. Add stock and cook,
covered, for 1 hour or until
tender on top of stove or in
oven, pre-set at 325°F or Mark 3.
Then lift the pieces of cooked
hare into a casserole for serving.
Strain the gravy into a pan, skim
off fat and add redcurrant jelly,
port and strained marinade.

Now make forcemeat balls :
melt butter in a pan, add onion,
cover and cook until soft but
not coloured. Mix breadcrumbs,
herbs and seasoning together
in a basin, add the onion and
enough beaten egg or milk to
bind. Shape mixture into small
balls, roll in seasoned flour,
then egg and crumb ; set aside
on a plate.

Boil gravy and reduce a little,
if necessary, to give a good
strong flavour. Draw aside and
stir in the blood mixed with the
arrowroot. Stir over heat until
it has the consistency of cream
but do not boil. Pour sauce over
the hare and reheat in the oven
for 5 minutes.

Watchpoint If the blood is
not available, kneaded butter
can be used to thicken the
sauce. The blood binds the
sauce together while the arrowroot helps to prevent it curdling.

Heat fat bath to 375°F, lower
in forcemeat on draining spoon
and fry until golden-brown.
Drain on absorbent paper. Then
serve with the hare.

Serve with red cabbage and creamed potatoes (see page 153)

Jugged hare is first marinated overnight and then braised ; redcurrant jelly and port are added to the gravy and the dish is served with forcemeat balls, braised red cabbage and creamed potatoes

Fricassée of hare with chestnuts

1 good-size hare (with blood)
few drops of vinegar
2-3 tablespoons olive oil
1½-2 fl oz brandy
1 small onion (sliced)
pepper (ground from mill)
½ lb pickled pork
1 oz butter
1 tablespoon plain flour
½ bottle red wine
salt and pepper
bouquet garni with stick of celery
1 clove of garlic (crushed)
½ lb button onions (blanched)
¼-¾ lb chestnuts
¼-¾ pint good stock (see page 155)

Method

Cut up the hare in small neat pieces (or have this done for you). Reserve the blood and add a few drops of vinegar to it to prevent it coagulating. Put the hare into a dish and sprinkle with the olive oil, brandy and onion. Grind over a little pepper, cover and leave to marinate for some hours, or overnight, either in a cool place or in the refrigerator.

Simmer the pork in water to cover for 30-40 minutes, cool slightly in the liquid, then take up and cut into cubes. Take the hare from the marinade and dab the pieces dry with absorbent paper. Brown the pieces lightly, using about 1 oz butter. Add the pork and, after a few minutes, stir in the flour. Pour on the wine, which should just cover the hare, season lightly and add the bouquet garni and the garlic. Bring to the boil, then cover and simmer very slowly on top of the stove, or put the pan in the oven (pre-set at 325°F or Mark 3) for 2½-3 hours. After 1 hour add the button onions and continue to cook until the hare and the onions are tender. Meanwhile scald and skin the chestnuts (see braised chestnuts, page 90), then simmer in good stock barely to cover for 35-40 minutes until tender.

At the end of the cooking time remove the bouquet garni and taste for seasoning. Add the reserved blood to the gravy in the pan as if it were a liaison. Bring to boiling point, but do not actually boil.

Dish up the hare and garnish with the chestnuts. Serve very hot.

Note : the hare will cook well in an enamelled iron casserole and the chestnuts can be added to it for serving. Should the liquid reduce rather too much, add a little additional stock, but this is best avoided.

Serve with creamed potatoes (see page 153) and small brussels sprouts.

Rabbit and bacon casserole

1 rabbit
dash of vinegar
2 tablespoons dripping
1 small onion (finely chopped)
1 tablespoon plain flour
$\frac{3}{4}$-1 pint stock (see page 155)
bouquet garni
1 rounded teaspoon tomato purée
1 clove of garlic (chopped)
salt and pepper
4 oz streaky bacon (in the piece)
12 pickling onions, or shallots

Method
Joint rabbit, trim and soak overnight in salted water with a dash of vinegar. Drain and dry well. Set oven at 350°F or Mark 4.

Brown joints slowly in hot dripping in a thick casserole. Add chopped onion, sprinkle in flour. Turn joints over to coat them in mixture and fry for 1 minute. Then draw aside, add enough stock barely to cover, add bouquet garni, purée and garlic. Season lightly, cover pan tightly and cook for 30 minutes in pre-set oven.

Meanwhile, cut bacon into short strips, blanch with pickling onions or shallots (put in cold water, bring to boil). Then drain and add to rabbit. Continue to cook for 1 hour or until all is tender. Remove bouquet garni, serve in casserole.

Casseroled rabbit with mustard

1-2 rabbits (jointed)
salt
$\frac{1}{4}$-$\frac{1}{2}$ lb streaky bacon, or pickled pork (in the piece)
2 tablespoons bacon fat, or dripping
4 onions (quartered)
1 tablespoon plain flour
1 pint stock (see page 155)
pepper (ground from mill)
bouquet garni
1 small carton ($2\frac{1}{2}$ fl oz) double cream, or evaporated milk
1 dessertspoon French mustard
1 dessertspoon chopped parsley

Wild rabbit is intended for this dish but tame rabbit can be used.

Method
Trim rabbit into neat joints, cutting wings (forelegs) in two and trimming off rib-cage. Soak the joints overnight in plenty of salted water with a dash of vinegar to remove the strong flavour. Then drain joints, rinse and dry thoroughly.

Cut away rind and rust (brown rim on underside) from bacon, or skin from the pork. Cut into large dice and blanch by putting into cold water, bringing to boil and simmering for 15-20 minutes. Then drain.

Heat fat in a thick casserole and lightly brown rabbit joints. Take out rabbit and put in bacon and onions ; fry well until coloured, draw aside, stir in flour and pour on stock. Bring to boil, add a little pepper, bouquet garni and rabbit joints. Cover casserole and cook for $1\frac{1}{2}$ hours, or until rabbit is really tender, in oven, pre-set at 350°F or Mark 4.

Draw aside, take out bouquet garni and add the cream mixed with mustard and parsley. Adjust seasoning and reheat.

Fricassée of rabbit

4-5 **pieces of Ostend rabbit, or 1**
   wild rabbit (jointed)
white stock (see page 156), or water
   (to cover meat)
2 onions (sliced)
1 bouquet garni
2 oz butter
3 tablespoons plain flour
$\frac{1}{4}$ **pint creamy milk**
2 oz button mushrooms

Method

Soak rabbit thoroughly in salted water, changing it from time to time. Blanch by putting into cold water, bringing to the boil, draining and refreshing. Trim away any pieces of skin with scissors and neaten the joints. Put rabbit into a shallow pan, barely cover with stock or water and add sliced onions.

For a more delicate flavour, blanch the onions first (by putting into cold water and bringing to the boil). Put in the bouquet garni, cover and simmer for 1-2 hours, or until very tender. Ostend (tame) rabbit takes less time than wild rabbit. Then drain off liquid, which should measure about $\frac{3}{4}$ pint.

Melt $1\frac{1}{2}$ oz butter in a saucepan, stir in flour off the heat, cook for about $\frac{1}{2}$ minute, cool a little and strain on the liquid. Blend and stir until boiling. Boil gently until it is the consistency of thick cream ; add the milk and continue cooking. At the same time, sauté the mushrooms in remaining butter in another pan. Add these to the sauce and pour it over the rabbit. Turn the fricassée into a covered dish and leave in a warm oven for 5 minutes before serving. This allows the flavour of the sauce to penetrate through the meat.

Rabbit paysanne

2 young rabbits (jointed)
2 oz plain flour (seasoned with salt, pepper and curry powder)
6 oz fat salt belly pork
2 large onions (thinly sliced)
6-8 oz streaky bacon rashers (No. 4 cut)
$\frac{1}{2}$ pint stock (see page 155), or $\frac{1}{4}$ pint dry cider and $\frac{1}{4}$ pint stock
2 tablespoons chopped parsley

Method

Trim rabbit joints and soak overnight in salted water.

Rinse and dry the joints thoroughly. Roll the joints in the seasoned flour, keeping at least 1 tablespoon in reserve to use as thickening. Cut pork into dice and put in a deep frying pan ; set on gentle heat to allow the fat to run. Then add onion, increase heat and fry gently until just coloured ; remove pork and onion from pan with a slice.

Wrap each rabbit joint in a whole rasher, or half, of bacon ; put into the pan and allow to brown slowly.

Watchpoint If the fat is insufficient when frying the rabbit joints, add a little dripping or lard.

Take rabbit out, put back pork and onions and set rabbit joints on top. Pour in a good $\frac{1}{4}$ pint stock (or cider), cover and simmer until tender (about 45 minutes). Then mix reserved flour (about 1 tablespoon) with about $\frac{1}{4}$ pint stock. Draw aside the pan and when off the boil pour in the stock and flour mixture, add parsley ; shake gently and reboil. Serve hot.

Dorset rabbit

2 small young rabbits
seasoned flour
6 oz streaky bacon rashers (unsmoked)
salt and pepper
2 tablespoons finely chopped fresh sage
$\frac{1}{2}$ cup milk

For forcemeat crust
1 lb onions (about 4)
2 oz butter
8 oz fresh white breadcrumbs
grated rind of $\frac{1}{2}$ lemon
3 rounded tablespoons chopped parsley
1 egg
little milk (optional)

Method

Joint rabbits and soak overnight in plenty of cold, strongly salted water.

Set oven at 325°F or Mark 3.

Drain, rinse and dry the joints thoroughly. Roll them in a little seasoned flour. Cut rind and rust from the bacon and cut into strips ; blanch and drain. Pack the joints into a deep ovenproof dish, seasoning well and sprinkling with the sage. Pour on the milk and scatter the bacon over the top.

To make forcemeat crust : chop the onions finely, cook in the butter until turning colour, then turn into a bowl. Let onion cool a little, then add the crumbs, lemon rind and parsley. Bind with the egg, adding a little milk if necessary, but be careful not to get mixture wet.

Spread forcemeat over rabbit and cook in pre-set oven for 2 hours, or until rabbit is tender and the top is browned. Cover with a piece of paper, if necessary, to prevent overbrowning.

Braised rabbit with tomatoes

1-2 young rabbits (depending on
size)
seasoned flour
4 oz salt belly pork (or thick
slice of green streaky bacon)
2 ½ fl oz oil
15 small pickling onions
scant ½ pint jellied stock (see page
155)
salt and pepper
2 tablespoons single cream
6 small tomatoes
pinch of caster sugar

Method

Soak the jointed rabbit in salted
water overnight.

Set oven at 350°F or Mark 4.
Dry joints thoroughly, then
roll them in seasoned flour.
Cut the pork into lardons. Heat
a cocotte with two-thirds of the
oil and add the lardons of pork.
Add the rabbit and colour
lightly on all sides. Then brown
the onions and add the stock ;
season and put in the pre-set
oven to cook for 50-60 minutes,
longer for an older rabbit. Baste
from time to time and allow the
stock to reduce almost to a
glaze during cooking. When
done, add the cream.

Scald and skin the tomatoes
(see page 156) and cut them in
half. Scoop out the seeds. Heat
the remaining oil in a frying pan
and when hot put in the tomatoes, cut side down ; when
coloured, turn, season, add the
sugar and cook until just brown.

Take up the rabbit. Test for
seasoning and pour sauce over
the rabbit. Garnish with the
tomatoes.

1 *Colouring floured rabbit joints in
oil with the lardons of pork*
2 *Arranging finished dish of the
braised rabbit with tomatoes*

Appendix

Notes and basic recipes

Aspic jelly

This is a jelly made from good fish, chicken, or meat stock very slightly sharpened with wine and a few drops of wine vinegar. Care must be taken that the stock is well flavoured and seasoned and that it is not too sharp, only pleasantly acidulated.

Aspic, when properly made, is excellent with fish or meat dishes, but unfortunately it is frequently disliked because it is unpleasantly sharp or tasteless. Aspic acts as a kind of preservative; food set in or brushed with aspic keeps its attractive appearance and finish for some hours.

With certain delicately-flavoured foods, such as fish, eggs or prawns, home-made aspic adds to and enhances the flavour. If you need aspic for brushing over sliced meat, use the commercially prepared variety, which is excellent for this — especially if a small quantity of the water is replaced by sherry. Make up according to directions on the packet or can.

Aspic, and most jellies containing wine, will keep for several days in the refrigerator. To do this, pour the liquid aspic into a jug, leave to set, then pour about $\frac{1}{2}$ inch cold water over the top, and refrigerate. Remember to pour water off before melting the aspic for use.

Basic aspic recipe

2 $\frac{1}{2}$ fl oz sherry
2 $\frac{1}{2}$ fl oz white wine
2 oz gelatine
1$\frac{3}{4}$ pints cold stock (see page 155)
1 teaspoon wine vinegar
2 egg whites

Method

Add wines to gelatine and set aside. Pour cold stock into scalded pan, add vinegar. Whisk egg whites to a froth, add them to the pan, set over moderate heat and whisk backwards until the stock is hot. Then add gelatine, which by now will have absorbed the wine, and continue whisking steadily until boiling point is reached.

Stop whisking and allow liquid to rise to the top of the pan; turn off heat or draw pan aside and leave to settle for about 5 minutes, then bring it again to the boil, draw pan aside once more and leave liquid to settle. At this point the liquid should look clear; if not, repeat the boiling-up process.

Filter the jelly through a scalded cloth. The aspic should be allowed to cool before use.

Breadcrumbs

To make white crumbs : take a large loaf (the best type to use is a sandwich loaf) at least two days old. Cut off the crust and keep to one side. Break up bread into crumbs either by rubbing through a wire sieve or a Mouli sieve, or by working in an electric blender.

Spread crumbs on to a sheet of paper laid on a baking tin and cover with another sheet of paper to keep of any dust. Leave to dry in a warm temperature — the plate rack, or warming drawer, or the top of the oven, or even the airing cupboard, is ideal. The crumbs may take a day or two to dry thoroughly, and they must be crisp before storing in a jar. To make them uniformly fine, sift them through a wire bowl strainer.

To make browned crumbs : bake the crusts in a slow oven until golden-brown, then crush or grind through a mincer. Sift and store as for white crumbs. These browned ones are known as raspings and are used for any dish that is coated with a sauce and browned in the oven.

Forcemeat balls

1 cup fresh white breadcrumbs
1 oz suet
salt and pepper
2 tablespoons chopped mixed herbs
  and parsley
1 small egg (beaten)

Method

Mix the crumbs and suet together, season well, add herbs and bind with the beaten egg. Roll this mixture into small balls and use as required.

Mayonnaise

2 egg yolks
salt and pepper
dry mustard
$\frac{3}{4}$ cup salad oil
2 tablespoons wine vinegar

This recipe will make $\frac{1}{2}$ pint of mayonnaise.

Method

Work egg yolks and seasonings with a small whisk or wooden spoon in a bowl until thick ; then start adding the oil drop by drop. When 2 tablespoons of oil have been added this mixture will be very thick. Now carefully stir in 1 teaspoon of the vinegar.

The remaining oil can then be added a little more quickly, either 1 tablespoon at a time and beaten thoroughly between each addition until it is absorbed, or in a thin steady stream if you are using an electric beater.

When all the oil has been absorbed, add remaining vinegar to taste, and extra salt and pepper as necessary.

To thin and lighten mayonnaise, add a little hot water. For a coating consistency, thin with a little cream or milk.

Eggs should not come straight from the refrigerator. If oil is cloudy or chilled, it can be slightly warmed which will lessen the chances of eggs curdling. Put oil bottle in a pan of hot water for a short time.

Watchpoint Great care must be taken to prevent mayonnaise curdling. Add oil drop by drop at first, and then continue adding it very slowly.

If mayonnaise curdles, start with a fresh yolk in another bowl and work well with seasoning, then add the curdled mixture to it very slowly and carefully. When curdled mixture is completely incorporated, more oil can be added if the mixture is too thin.

Mornay (cheese) sauce

$\frac{1}{2}$ pint milk
1 slice onion
1 small bayleaf
6 peppercorns
1 blade of mace
$\frac{3}{4}$ oz butter
1 rounded tablespoon plain flour
1-1$\frac{1}{2}$ oz (2-3 rounded tablespoons)
  grated cheese
$\frac{1}{2}$ teaspoon made mustard (French
  or English)

Serve with eggs, fish, chicken and vegetables.

The cheese can be a mixture of Gruyère and Parmesan or a dry Cheddar. If using Gruyère, which thickens sauce, reduce basic roux to $\frac{1}{2}$ oz each butter and flour (1 tablespoon). If too thick, add a little milk.

Method

Pour milk into a saucepan, add the flavourings, cover pan and infuse on gentle heat for 5-7 minutes. Strain milk and set it aside. Rinse and wipe out the pan and melt the butter in it. Remove from heat and blend in the flour then cook gently until straw coloured.

Pour on half the milk and blend until smooth using a wooden spoon, then add rest of milk. Return to a slow to moderate heat and stir until boiling. Boil for no longer than 2 minutes.

Remove from heat and gradually stir in grated cheese. When well mixed, add mustard. Reheat but do not boil.

Onions, glazed

Cover the onions with cold water, add salt and bring to the boil. Tip off the water, add 1-1½ oz butter and a dusting of caster sugar. Cover and cook gently until golden-brown on all sides and cooked through (about 10 minutes).

Pastry

Flaky pastry

8 oz plain flour
pinch of salt
3 oz butter
3 oz lard
¼ pint ice-cold water (to mix)

Method

Sift the flour with salt into a bowl. Divide the fats into four portions (two of butter, two of lard) ; rub one portion — either lard or butter — into the flour and mix to a firm dough with cold water. The amount of water varies with different flour but an average quantity for 8 oz flour is 4-5 fluid oz (about ¼ pint or 8-10 tablespoons) ; the finer the flour the more water it will absorb.

Knead the dough lightly until smooth, then roll out to an oblong. Put a second portion of fat (not the same kind as first portion rubbed in) in small pieces on to two-thirds of the dough. Fold in three, half turn dough to bring the open edge towards you and roll out again to an oblong. Put on a third portion of fat in pieces, fold dough in three,

wrap in a cloth or polythene bag and leave in a cool place for 15 minutes.

Roll out dough again, put on remaining fat in pieces, fold and roll as before. If pastry looks at all streaky, give one more turn and roll again.

Note :

To bake blind Chill pastry case, line with crumpled greaseproof paper and three-parts fill with uncooked rice or beans. An 8-inch diameter flan ring holding a 6-8 oz quantity of pastry should cook for about 26 minutes in an oven at 400°F or Mark 6. Take out paper and beans for last 5 minutes baking.

Puff pastry

8 oz plain flour
pinch of salt
8 oz butter
1 teaspoon lemon juice
scant ¼ pint water (ice cold)

Method

Sift flour and salt into a bowl. Rub in a piece of butter the size of a walnut. Add lemon juice to water, make a well in centre of flour and pour in about two-thirds of the liquid. Mix with a palette, or round-bladed, knife. When the dough is beginning to form, add remaining water.

Turn out the dough on to a marble slab, a laminated-plastic work top, or a board, dusted with flour. Knead dough for 2-3 minutes, then roll out to a square about ½-¾ inch thick.

Beat butter, if necessary, to make it pliable and place in centre of dough. Fold this up over butter to enclose it completely (sides and ends over centre like a parcel). Wrap in a cloth or piece of grease-proof paper and put in the refrigerator for 10-15 minutes.

Flour slab or work top, put on

dough, the join facing upwards, and bring rolling pin down on to dough 3-4 times to flatten it slightly.

Now roll out to a rectangle about $\frac{1}{2}$-$\frac{3}{4}$ inch thick. Fold into three, ends to middle, as accurately as possible, if necessary pulling the ends to keep them rectangular. Seal the edges with your hand or rolling pin and turn pastry half round to bring the edge towards you. Roll out again and fold in three (keep a note of the 'turns' given). Set pastry aside in refrigerator for 15 minutes.

Repeat this process twice, giving a total of 6 turns with a 15 minute rest after each two turns. Then leave in the refrigerator until wanted.

Rich shortcrust pastry

8 oz plain flour
pinch of salt
6 oz butter
1 rounded dessertspoon caster sugar (for sweet pastry)
1 egg yolk
2-3 tablespoons cold water

Method
Sift the flour with a pinch of salt into a mixing bowl. Drop in the butter and cut it into the flour until the small pieces are well coated. Then rub them in with the fingertips until the mixture looks like fine breadcrumbs. Stir in the sugar, mix egg yolk with water, tip into the fat and flour and mix quickly with a palette knife to a firm dough.

Turn on to a floured board and knead lightly until smooth. If possible, chill in refrigerator (wrapped in greaseproof paper, a polythene bag or foil) for 30 minutes before using.

Shortcrust pastry for raised pies

8 oz plain flour
$\frac{1}{2}$ teaspoon salt

4 oz butter, or butter and lard (mixed)
1 small egg
2-3 tablespoons cold water

Method
Sift the flour and salt together on a pastry board or table. Make a well in the centre and in this place the fat, egg and water. Work up together, starting in the centre and gradually drawing in flour. Work until smooth, then chill for 2 hours or longer.

Potatoes

Château potatoes
1 lb old or new potatoes
1-2 oz butter
salt

Method
Old potatoes should be blanched before browning. Cut peeled potatoes into quarters lengthways, then use a potato peeler to trim off sharp edges. Blanch, drain and dry. If using new potatoes, scrape and leave them whole. Wash and dry potatoes thoroughly, but do not blanch.

Melt butter in a casserole, add potatoes and cook over a moderate heat until golden-brown, shaking casserole occasionally to stop them from sticking. Season lightly, cover and put into oven to finish cooking for 10-12 minutes at 400°F or Mark 6.

Creamed potatoes
1$\frac{1}{2}$ lb old potatoes
1-2 oz butter
$\frac{1}{4}$ pint milk
salt and pepper

Even good cooks fall down on mashed potatoes, particularly when entertaining, as they will dish them up too early and have to keep them hot. The potatoes then get an unattractive yellow skin. To prepare early and keep them hot, cook as follows.

Method

Cut the peeled potatoes in even-size pieces if very large, and put into cold salted water. Bring to the boil and cook until tender (about 20 minutes). Test with the point of a fine knife or trussing needle ; do not test with the thick prongs of a fork or the potato will break.

Watchpoint Take care to cook potatoes in water and not let it boil away from them.

When potatoes are tender, tilt the lid of the pan and pour off all the water. Return to a gentle heat and, with the lid half-closed, continue cooking a few minutes until the potatoes are dry. Then add the butter — as much as you like — and crush the potatoes with a potato masher or a fork. Adjust seasoning. Press them down firmly to the bottom of the saucepan and pour over boiling milk ($\frac{1}{4}$ pint is enough for 1$\frac{1}{2}$-2 lb potatoes). Do not stir, but put the lid on the saucepan which should stand in a hot place until your main course is dished up. Creamed potatoes can be kept hot in this way for up to 30 minutes, and the potatoes will absorb the milk on standing. Just before dishing up, beat the potatoes very well with a wooden spoon, or small electric whisk, until fluffy.

Red cabbage, braised

1$\frac{1}{2}$-2 lb red cabbage (finely shredded)
1 onion (sliced)
1 oz butter
2 cooking apples (peeled and sliced)
2-3 tablespoons wine vinegar
1 rounded tablespoon sugar
salt and pepper

1 oz kneaded butter (twice as much butter as flour, worked into a paste)

Method

Wash and quarter the cabbage, cut out the stalk and shred finely. Put into a large pan of boiling water, cook 1 minute only, then drain well. (The cabbage will turn a deep violet at this point but when the vinegar is added later it returns to its original colour.)

Slice the onion and cook in the butter until soft but not coloured. Peel and slice the apples, add to the onion and continue cooking 2-3 minutes. Turn out on to a plate.

Add the cabbage to the pan, layering with the apple mixture and sprinkling with the vinegar, 2-3 tablespoons water, sugar and seasoning. Cover with buttered paper and lid and cook in a slow oven for 1$\frac{1}{2}$ -2 hours at 325°F or Mark 3. Stir from time to time and moisten with a little extra water, or stock, if necessary.

When very tender stir in the kneaded butter a small piece at a time, adding enough to bind the cabbage and juices. Adjust the seasoning.

This cabbage is even better cooked the day before, and then reheated just before serving.

Redcurrant jelly

It is not possible to give a specific quantity of redcurrants as the recipe is governed by the amount of juice made, which is variable.

Method

Wash the fruit and, without removing from the stems, put in a 7 lb jam jar or stone crock Cover and stand in deep pan of hot water. Simmer on top of the stove or in the oven at 350°F or Mark 4, mashing the fruit a little from time to time, until all the juice is extracted (about 1 hour).

Then turn fruit into a jelly bag or double linen strainer, and allow to drain undisturbed overnight over a basin.

Watchpoint To keep the jelly clear and sparkling, do not try to speed up the draining process by forcing juice through ; this will only make the jelly cloudy.

Now measure juice. Allowing 1 lb lump or preserving sugar to each pint of juice, mix juice and sugar together, dissolving over slow heat. When dissolved, bring to the boil, boil hard for 3-5 minutes and skim with a wooden spoon. Test a little on a saucer : allow jelly to cool, tilt saucer and, if jelly is set, it will wrinkle. Put into jam jars place small circles of greaseproof paper over jelly, label and cover with jam pot covers. Store in a dry larder until required.

Rice salad
10 oz long grain rice
3 oz pistachio nuts
$\frac{1}{4}$ pint French dressing (see method)
$\frac{1}{4}$ teaspoon ground cinnamon
salt and pepper
3 oz currants

Method
Cook the rice in plenty of salted water for 10-12 minutes, drain and rinse with hot water. Leave rice to drain again, then turn it on to a large flat dish and allow to dry. Blanch, split and shred pistachio nuts.

Prepare the French dressing, using three parts of oil to one part of wine vinegar and mixing the cinnamon with the salt and pepper.

Mix currants, rice and pistachio nuts together and moisten with the French dressing. Season with extra salt and pepper, if necessary.

Stocks

Bouillon cubes
In a emergency a bouillon cube can be used for certain dishes, but it can never replace properly-made stock because it will lack the characteristic jellied quality. Bouillon cubes are salty and there is always the danger of overdoing the seasoning.

Brown bone stock
3 lb beef bones (or mixed beef / veal)
2 onions (quartered)
2 carrots (quartered)
1 stick of celery
large bouquet garni
6 peppercorns
3-4 quarts water
salt

6-quart capacity saucepan, or small fish kettle

Method
Wipe bones but do not wash unless unavoidable. Put into a very large pan. Set on gentle heat and leave bones to fry gently for 15-20 minutes. Enough fat will come out from the marrow so do not add any to pan unless bones are very dry.

After 10 minutes add the vegetables, having sliced the celery into 3-4 pieces.

When bones and vegetables are just coloured, add herbs, peppercorns, salt and water, which should come up two-thirds above level of ingredients. Bring slowly to the boil, skimming occasionally, then half cover pan to allow reduction to take place and simmer 4-5 hours, or until stock tastes strong and good.

Strain off and use bones again for a second boiling. Although this second stock will not be so strong as the first, it is good for soups and gravies. Use the first stock for brown sauces, sautés, casseroles, or where a jellied stock is required. For a strong beef broth, add 1 lb shin of beef to the pot halfway through the cooking.

Chicken stock

This should ideally be made from the giblets (neck, gizzard, heart and feet, if available), but never the liver which imparts a bitter flavour. This is better kept for making pâté, or sautéd and used as a savoury. Dry fry the giblets with an onion, washed but not peeled, and cut in half. To dry fry, use a thick pan with a lid, with barely enough fat to cover the bottom. Allow the pan to get very hot before putting in the giblets and onion, cook on full heat until lightly coloured. Remove pan from heat before covering with 2 pints of cold water. Add a large pinch of salt, a few peppercorns and a bouquet garni (bay leaf, thyme, parsley) and simmer gently for 1-2 hours. Alternatively, make the stock when you cook the chicken by putting the giblets in the roasting tin around the chicken with the onion and herbs, and use the measured quantity of water.

White bone stock

This stock forms a basis for cream sauces, white stews, etc. It is made in the same way as brown bone stock, except that bones and vegetables are not browned before the water is added and veal bones are used. Do not add the vegetables until the bones have come to the boil and the fat has been skimmed off the liquid.

Vegetable stock

1 lb carrots (quartered)
1 lb onions (quartered)
½ head of celery (sliced)
½ oz butter
3-4 peppercorns

1 teaspoon tomato purée
2 quarts water
salt

Method
Quarter vegetables, brown lightly in the butter in a large pan. Add peppercorns, tomato purée, water and salt. Bring to boil, cover pan and simmer 2 hours or until the stock has a good flavour.

Tomatoes

To skin tomatoes : place them in a bowl, scald by pouring boiling water over them, count 12, then pour off the hot water and replace it with cold. The skin then comes off easily.

To remove seeds : slice off the top of each tomato and flick out seeds with the handle of a teaspoon, use bowl of spoon to detach core.

Wine for cooking

Both red and white wines are best reduced before adding to a dish or sauce, the exception being white wine when it is added with a quantity of water for poaching fish.

This reduction mellows and concentrates the flavour and takes away the alcohol. This applies particularly to red wine, which is brought to the boil and boiled rapidly until reduced by about an eighth. During this time the wine may catch alight if you are cooking in a shallow pan over a naked flame, in which case allow it to burn out; the wine will then be ready for you to use.

White wine is reduced even more than red for adding to a sauce, the amount being stated in recipes.

Wine for cooking is measured by the size of glass from which it is traditionally served : red and white wines — 4 fl oz
sherry, port, madeira, marsala — 2 ½ fl oz.

Glossary

Baste To spoon hot fat / liquid over food as it roasts.

Blanch To whiten meats and remove strong tastes from vegetables by bringing to boil from cold water and draining before further cooking. Green vegetables should be put into boiling water and cooked for up to 1 minute.

Bouquet garni Traditionally a bunch of parsley, thyme, bayleaf, for flavouring stews and sauces. Other herbs can be added. Remove before serving dish.

Butter, clarified Butter cleared by heating gently until foaming, skimming well, straining off clear yellow oil, leaving sediment (milk solids) behind.

Butter, kneaded A liaison for thickening. Twice as much butter as flour is worked into a paste on a plate with a fork, and added in small pieces to the cooled mixture off the heat. Butter melts and draws the flour into the liquid.

Cocotte 'En cocotte' implies that the food is cooked and served in the same round or oval ovenproof dish.

Croûte Small round of bread, lightly toasted or fried, spread or piled up with a savoury mixture, also used as a garnish. Not to be confused with pie or bread crust (also croûte). Sometimes used to describe decorative shapes, eg. of aspic.

Deglaze To heat stock and / or wine together with flavoursome sediments left in roasting / frying pan so that gravy / sauce is formed. (Remove excess fat first).

Dry frying An alternative to grilling. Take a thick, heavy frying pan. Set on full heat for a few minutes, then put in 1 tablespoon oil or dripping and after a few seconds put in meat. Keep on full heat until well browned on one side, pressing food well down with a palette knife ; then turn and brown other side. Lower heat if necessary to complete cooking.

Flour, seasoned Flour to which salt and pepper have been added.

Infuse To steep in liquid (not always boiling) in warm place to draw flavour into the liquid.

Julienne 1 A clear vegetable soup to which a mixture of finely shredded vegetables has been added.
2 The cut size and shape of vegetables and garnishes for certain dishes. A julienne strip is usually about $\frac{1}{8}$ inch by 1$\frac{1}{2}$-2 inches long.

Lardons Small $\frac{1}{4}$ inch thick strips of fat about 1$\frac{1}{2}$ inches long, cut from a piece of larding bacon, which is solid fat. They are used to give extra fat to cuts of meat that have little or none of their own to protect them from drying out during cooking. These strips are larded, or sewn, into the meat with a larding needle.

Liaison Mixture for thickening / binding sauce / gravy / soup, e.g. roux, egg yolks and cream, kneaded butter. Liaisons should be blended in gradually, away from the heat.

Marinate To soak raw meat / game / fish in cooked or raw spiced liquid (marinade) of wine, oil, herbs and vegetables for hours / days before cooking. This softens, tenderises and flavours and a marinade can be used for final sauce. Use glass / glazed / enamel / stainless steel vessel to withstand effects of acid.

157

Index

Reduce To boil down sauce, or any liquid, to concentrate flavour and thicken the consistency.

Refresh To pour cold water over previously blanched and drained food. This sets vegetable colours, cleans meat / offal.

Roux Fat and flour liaison. This is the basis of all flour sauces. The weight of fat should generally be slightly more than that of flour. To make, melt fat, stir in flour (off heat) and pour on water / stock / milk. Stir until roux thickens, bring to boil and cook.

Rust Underside of bacon rasher or ham, on the side opposite to the rind. It is often tough and strong flavoured, so should be cut off.

Sauté To brown food in butter or oil and butter. Sometimes cooking is completed in a 'small' sauce — ie. one made on the food in the sauté pan.

Scald 1 To plunge into boiling water for easy peeling.
2 To heat a liquid eg. milk, to just under boiling point.

Slake To mix arrowroot / cornflour with a little cold water before adding to a liquid for thickening.

Sweat To draw out flavour by cooking diced or sliced vegetables gently in a little melted butter in covered pan until softened (5-10 minutes).